SQUIRRELS

The fox squirrel is the most common tree squirrel found in Colorado. It thrives in a variety of tree habitats from forest to suburban areas.   Fox squirrels are about one and a half feet long if you count the tail and will weigh about a pound. The top of the body is covered with dark grey fur. A lighter grey fur covers the underside of the body.

Squirrels are most active early in the morning and late evening. They can move adeptly on both the ground and in trees. Their diet consists of nuts, seeds and fruits.

Squirrels bury nuts for winter food supply by digging holes in the ground with their front feet. They have a keen sense of smell and are capable of locating buried nuts by smell under a foot of snow.

Fox squirrels live in dens or nests which are built in trees. Old wood pecker holes or natural tree cavities serve as dens. Nest are constructed of twigs and leaves packed together to offer protection against the weather.

They move through trees by leaping from branch to branch. Their bushy tail provides some lift when they leap. The tail also serves as an effective blanket during the winter.   Mating occurs in mid-winter. Two to three young are born in the spring. A second litter may be born in the summer.

REGULATIONS

Squirrel season opens in mid-September with the start of the small game season. The season runs until the end of February. The daily bag limit is five animals. There are some specific rules that apply to certain areas. Make sure you check the small game regulations before hunting.

HOW TO HUNT SQUIRRELS

The middle of October is the best time to start hunting squirrels. Hunting these animals in the early season is relatively easy. As the season progresses, squirrels develop a wariness about hunters.

By late fall, they can be a challenge to even the most experienced hunter. Squirrels react to hunting pressure as do other animals. The sound of gunfire, hunters in the woods and the general disruption of their habitat brings out a natural wariness.

Successful squirrel hunters learn to change their tactics as the season progresses. In the early part of the season, you can effectively find squirrels by walking through forested areas. Later in the season, stalking and stand-hunting will become more effective.

Stalking can be most effective when you hear the distant chatter which is typical of fox squirrels. Getting close enough for a shot can be challenging. It's almost impossible to move quietly in a leaf-littered forest floor. If you can find a trail that is relatively free of forest clutter, you should be able to move quietly.

An ideal time to hunt squirrels is after a good rain or snow. The leaves are wet or covered with snow so you can walk through them quietly. Squirrels seem to linger longer in foul weather.

Floating down a Colorado river or stream that is lined with trees is another way to hunt winter squirrels. Duck and squirrel hunting make good combination hunts. If you are interested in combination float hunts, read our chapter on duck hunting for more helpful information.

WHERE TO HUNT SQUIRRELS

Fortunately, finding a place to squirrel hunt in Colorado isn't difficult. The Division of Wildlife owns and leases a number of properties along prime river bottoms. The best hunting is in eastern Colorado.

The South Platte River northeast of Fort Morgan heads the list of the best areas to hunt. The Bonny Reservoir State Recreation Area 200 miles east of Denver is another popular spot. Hunt the trees that line the shoreline of the lake. The area below the dam is also good.

The south central part of the state offers good squirrel hunting out of Alamosa. Alamosa Canyon and Mineral Hot Springs in the San Luis Valley are two of the best areas. Fort Collins hunters can find squirrels in Cherokee Park northeast of town. The park is just below the Red Feathers lakes.

CHAPTER 8

TURKEY HUNTING

The wild turkey is the largest North American game bird. A full grown tom turkey will weigh up to 25 pounds. The females are smaller and trimmer than the males. Although wild turkeys resemble their domestic cousins, they are more stream lined with a longer neck, tail and legs.

The feathers of the neck, chest and back are black and brown accompanied by a chestnut brown tail. The colors of the females are not as bright as the males.

The head of a tom is covered with fleshy growths which hang over the bill and down the neck. Gobblers also have a growth of feathers which sprout from the middle of the breast and is called a beard. One out of 20 hens will grow a beard.

Wild turkeys will form flocks of from 10 to 20 birds. As a group, they'll feed together on seeds, berries, grasses and insects. At night, they roost in trees to avoid predators.

If disturbed, they prefer to run from danger rather than fly. They can cover 18 miles of rough terrain in an hour. If they choose to fly, they are capable of extremely rapid takeoffs.

REGULATIONS

Colorado has a spring and fall turkey season. The spring season runs from mid-April through May. The fall season starts in mid-September and ends in mid-October.

The big difference between the two seasons is the ''beard turkey only'' requirement in the spring. You can only use shotguns in the spring. Rifles are allowed in the fall.

There are a number of limited game management areas which can be hunted by obtaining special permits. Obtain a permit by sending an ''Unlimited Permit Application'' to the Colorado Division of Wildlife. Applications forms are included in the ''Colorado Hunting Information Folder for Turkeys'' available at sport shops.

If you choose not to apply for a ''limited permit,'' you may apply for an ''unlimited permit.'' This entitles hunting anywhere in the state that has not been designated as a limited or closed area.

HOW TO HUNT TURKEYS

In theory, turkey hunting is easy. The big tom is called in with a hen-like noise. The tom struts near your blind, and ''BANG,'' you've got your bird. In reality, by the time a tom reaches maturity in two years, he will have seen and heard just about everything you have to offer.

If you want to put some consistency into your turkey hunts, you're going to need to solicit every legal tool and technique you can to lure a bird within range. This includes everything from calls to camouflage.

For starters, select a good call that fits your needs. The traditional box call is a favorite device among veteran turkey callers. Although this all wood call is great for reproducing natural wild turkey sounds, its' pitch changes with humidity.

To overcome the humidity factor, turkey call manufactures came up with a natural slate and cedar peg friction call box. Sound from the slate is generated by sliding the cedar peg across the surface. The device reproduces sounds comparable to the box call but consistently works well during high humidity conditions.

There is also a diaphragm call that fits onto the roof of the mouth. Effective turkey calls are produced when air is blown through a reed mounted in back of the diaphragm.

All of the calls which we have discussed are good. Select the one that you're most comfortable with and practice until your calls are exactly right for every hunting situation.

Learn how to start calling with clear yelps, clucks, cackles, purrs and whines. You can buy or rent video tapes which will help you perfect your calls.

Complete camouflage is as important to turkey hunting success as the calling technique. Wild turkeys have only a mediocre sense of smell. They more than make up for this short-coming with a keen eyesight. The camouflage outfit should include a head or face net, gloves, shirt and pants plus netting for the blind.

Turkey hunting has no place for shiny objects. Nothing will make an approaching gobbler turn and run faster than the sun reflecting off a shiny gun barrel or polished wood stock. Wrap your gun in camouflage tape to avoid the problem.

The next step in preparing for the hunt is to learn about the movement patterns of Colorado gobblers. In the early morning, they will fly down their tree roost to the stream and river bottoms. From there, they'll move up the sides of the hills to the tops of the mesas by mid-afternoon. In the evening, the flock will move back down to the stream and river bottoms. By nightfall, they'll be back in their tree roost.

Coordinate your calling duels around the movement of the turkeys. If you are calling birds that are in roost, set-up your blind about 200 yards from the roost at least a half hour before daylight.

Plan your evening hunt to take advantage of the fact that the birds will in all probability return to the same roost. Select the best available cover you can about 200 yards from the roost. Shooting near a roost will force the birds to find another roost. If you make this mistake, you'll have to start your ''roost scouting'' all over again.

You can improve the odds of pulling a wary gobbler to within range by using a decoy. There are a couple of techniques for using decoys. One approach is to locate a gobbler with your call and then place a decoy in the area you want to steer the gobbler to.

The second approach is to place your decoy about 100 yards from a known roost. Do this as quietly as you can, an hour before daylight. If the birds hear you, they will not fly down your way.

Once your decoy is in place, make a few hen yelp calls. If you perform the ritual properly, you should first get a flock of hens moving toward your call. This is exactly what you want to happen. The tom that you've been looking for can't be far behind.

WHERE TO HUNT TURKEYS

Turkey hunting in Colorado has improved dramatically over the last ten years, thanks to the aggressive game management programs of the Division of Wildlife. The southern half of the state supports the best hunting areas.

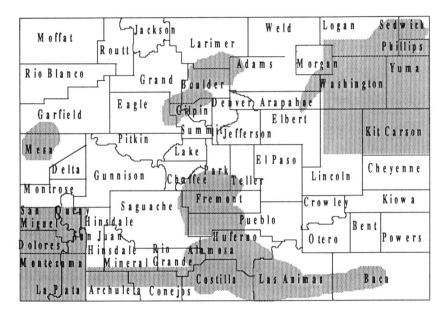

T O P   T U R K E Y   H U N T I N G   S P O T S

Wild turkeys are not native to northeastern Colorado. However, the Division of Wildlife has successfully planted Rio Grande turkeys in the dense river bottom regions.

Most of the hunting in the northeast is controlled by limited permits. The smallest area is located in the Colorado Springs Wildlife park along Fountain Creek. The South Platte and Republican River drainages are considered the top spots.

There is a growing population of birds along the South Platte River in Logan and Morgan counties. Most of this area is open on a limited permit basis. Check the hunting regulations for the most current information. The front range in Latimer County supports a good population of birds.

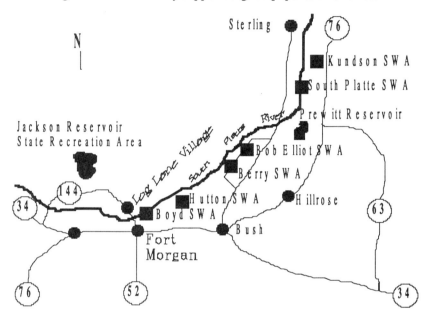

The area west of Delores is another good spot. Turkeys have been heavily transplanted into this area over the past five years and they are doing very well. There is good hunting along the Delores River starting from just below McPhee Reservoir down to Delores Canyon.

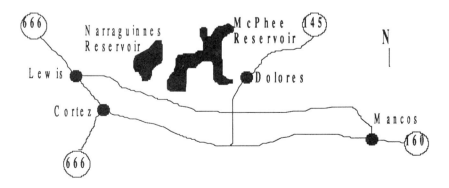

All of the drainages running into the Delores River from the north are good areas to hunt. The Glade, Beaver, Plateau and House Creek areas are worth checking out. Further to the east, hunting is good up on the West Fork of the Delores River in Haycamp Mesa.

All of the area south of Colorado Springs to the New Mexico border is good. The closer you get to the border, the better it gets. The "hot spots" are in the areas around the towns of Wetmore, Greenwood, Bealah, Rye, Green-horn, Apache City, Gardner, Bradford, Russell, LaVeta, Aguilar and Monument Park.

The Colorado Springs area has plenty of public land to hunt in the San Isabel and Pike National Forests. It's tough to get into theses areas for the spring hunt because of the snow pack. You should have no problems in the fall.

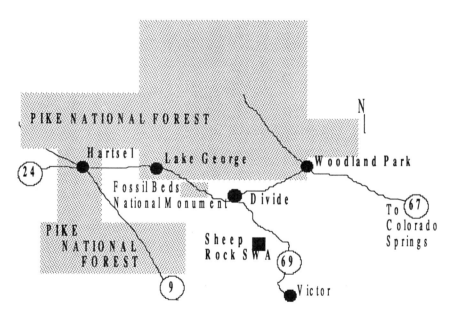

Public hunting for turkey is available in the San Isabel National Forest. If you can obtain access to private land in the area, so much the better. Chaffee Creek SWA is 13 miles north of Buena Vista off Highway 24. This 350 acre park includes the 150 acre Chaffee Reservoir. There are camping facilities within the park which also offers easy access into the San Isabel National Forest.

There are a good number of birds in the Tarryall Reservoir area. Try the south slopes of the Tarryall Mountains. The South Platte below Decker is a good area for Denver metro hunters. There is a great deal of dense growth along some of the creek drainages which feed into the river. This is classic turkey habitat.

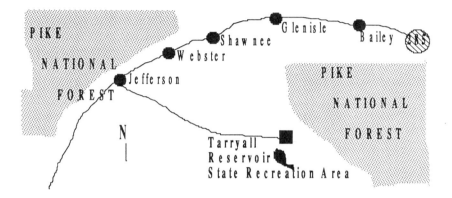

The western side of the state offers good hunting around Pagosa Springs. The birds in the area are down low and along the roads. They'll move up into the higher elevations and inaccessible creek drainages after the start of the season to avoid the hunting pressure. Plan your hunt at the higher elevations of Fourmile, McCabe and Turkey Creek drainages. It's good hunting if you are willing to make the hike.

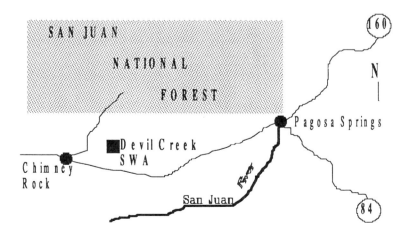

Grand Mesa supports a fair population of turkeys. The best hunting is in the lower valleys around Molina and Collbran. Unfortunately, most of the land here is private. The Uncompahgre Plateau region was closed a couple of years ago to protect a transplant program. It will be a great area to hunt when it opens.

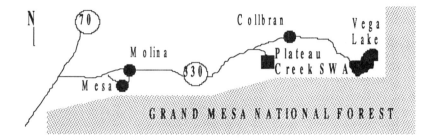

There is good hunting along the Purgatorie River out of Los Animias if you can get access through the private land. The area west of Trinidad and I-25 in Huerfano County is another good hunting spot. The canyons along both sides of the Arkansas River from Coaldale to Parkdale support a good population of birds.

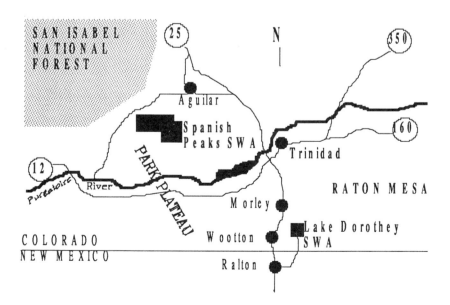

The Republican drainage is divided into two units. The Bonney Reservoir area is the most popular. Most of the prime habitat is in the South Republican State Wildlife Area. All of this is open to public hunting.

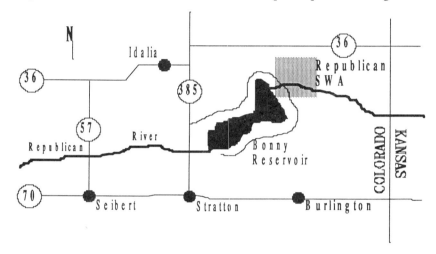

The lower end of the reservoir feeds into the Republican River which windes its' way southwest all the way to Lincoln County. Most of the prime turkey habitat is found along the banks and drainages of the Republican. Look for the scrub oak bushes which produce small acorns. Acorns are a favorite food of turkeys. These brush areas provide consistent feeding grounds for turkeys.

Hunters should set up blinds in the oak brush areas for early morning calling. The birds will typically come down off the roosts in the morning and head for water at the rivers edge. From there, they will work their way back up into the hills by feeding on acorns and seeds as they go.

If your blind is in the propper location and well concealed, you should get an opportunity to catch turkeys either going to or comming from water. These birds will folllow the same water and feed route every day if they haven't been seriously disturbed by other hunters or predators. If you find a lot of sign in one general area, you may be on your way to landing a big gobbler.

As a side note, this same strech of the Republican River offers some of the states finest pheasant hunting. It also provides excellent habitat for squirrel and rabbits. It is a perfect area for those hunter that enjoy "jump shooting" ducks. And, Bonny Reservoir is one of the best winter hunting areas for both ducks and geese.   Use your turkey hunt as an opportunity to scout out other hunting options in the area.

There are a number of State Wildlife Areas that extend   along the South Platte River from Fort Morgan to Sterling. There are several state properties along the river which are open to the public.

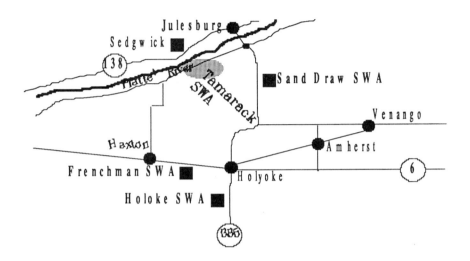

CHAPTER 9

UPLAND GAME BIRDS

DOVES

Doves are a familiar bird throughout North American. Their range extends from Canada through the continental United States, Mexico and South America.

These birds will measure 11 inches in length if you count their 6 inch tail. The prevailing color of this member of the pigeon family is grayish-blue. The coloring of the male and female are the same. The song of the dove is a distinctive mourning sound. Hence, these birds have been given the nickname of "Mourning Dove".

Doves are migratory birds. The prefer to stay in the northern states during the summer which is also their breeding period. Doves produce as many as 3 or 4 hatches before they head south in the fall.

The female constructs a nest made of twigs. Two eggs are laid and will hatch in two weeks. The young are born completely without feathers. The parents will nourish the young on "pigeon's milk". Seeds and insects are consumed by the adult birds and processed into liquid which is fed back to the young.

Mourning doves are shy birds. Couples will remain together and tend to stay away from other doves. They will come together as a group in common feeding and watering areas.

REGULATIONS

Dove season opens the first of September and lasts through October. The bag limit is 15 birds with no more than 30 in possession. Most hunters prefer to use 12 to 20 gauge shotguns. A number 6 or 8 shot size is common.

HOW TO HUNT DOVES

Doves are creatures of habit. They fly out in the morning to water and feed. They will roost in trees at night and prefer trees with open branches. If they are not disturbed, they will return to the same watering, feeding, and roosting spots daily.

As soon as the sun comes up, doves head for water. They prefer watering spots that are open with a power line or dead tree near by for a sentry spot. One or two guards will be posted to assure the safety of the rest.

The birds will mill around the water for about an hour before they take off for their favorite feeding spot. Look for dove in wheat stubble, fields with sunflowers; or wild grasses and any watering spot that is close to an obvious feeding area.

Scouting is essential if you plan to hunt doves. Go to the water early in the morning and then move out into the open fields by mid-morning. Look for the birds to move into shaded areas by mid-day. Move back into their roosting area in the evening.

Watch the patterns of the birds as they fly in and out of the different areas. Note the time of the flight pattern and plan your hunt accordingly. Pick your spot and start shooting.

WHERE TO HUNT DOVES

Dove hunting is generally good throughout the state. Look for the better hunting to be along the major rivers and reservoirs. This is particularly true in a dry year.

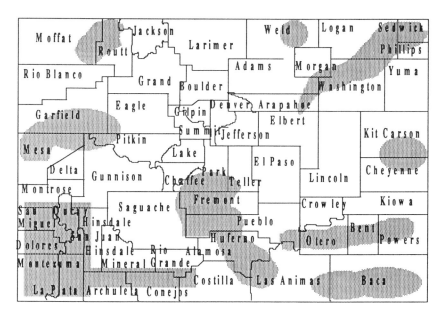

TOP DOVE HUNTING SPOTS

The Pawnee National Grasslands north of Greely offers good dove hunting if the weather cooperates. The key to success in this area is to first find water. That can be a difficult task in a dry year. If you can find a pothole of water, you will have found yourself a good spot to hunt.

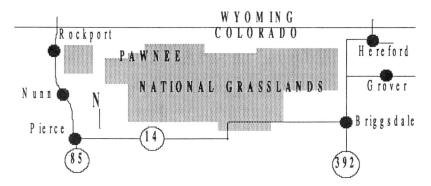

There is a spot that usually has water just east of the town of Briggsdale. Take highway 14 east of town and turn north on County Road 98. Everything on both sides of the road for several miles is public land.

You will run into some irrigation ditches along this road which are excellent to hunt. There is creek called Wild Horse Creek that crosses the road about three miles in. If it's not dry, start looking for doves in the creek beds.

Make sure you take your binoculars with you when you hunt the Grasslands. If you see birds moving in and out of an area, get over there and find out where their water is. Find a hiding spot and wait for the doves to come to you.

Trinidad Lake SWA is one of the better dove spots to hunt. The best shooting is in the Rielly Canyon access area which is on the northwest side of the lake.

Next try the lower Arkansas Valley and John Martin SWA. The best hunting is above the reservoir on the river. John Martin is west of the town of Lamar.

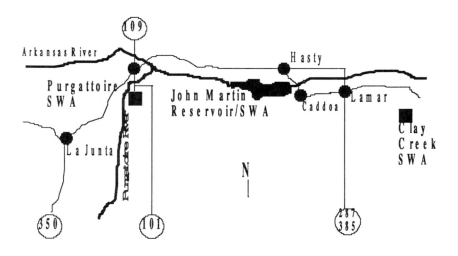

The Western Slope is not to be overlooked when it comes to dove hunting. Hunting in the lower Grand Valley below Grand Junction and any of the many rivers and streams in the area are excellent. Highline Reservoir SRA offers plenty of public land to hunt. Highline is north of Loma off highway 139.

Rio Grande SWA is one of the more popular public hunting spots in the San Luis Valley. The area is located a couple of miles east of Monte Vista. The southwest end of the San Luis Valley offers good shooting at Hot Creek SWA. It doesn't get anywhere near the pressure the Rio Grande does.

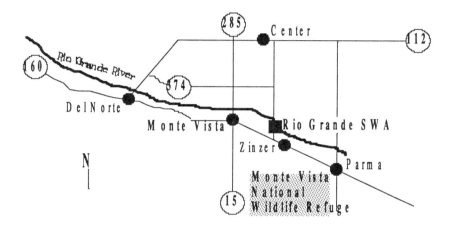

The southeast corner of the state really begins to turn on in the latter part of the season. The public land in Two Buttes SWA holds plenty of doves. The area is two miles north of the Baca/Powers county line on U.S. 287.

GROUSE

Blue grouse are the most under-hunted game birds in Colorado. An yet, they are one of the most popular game birds to hunt in the southern and eastern states.

These birds are about 18 inches long and will weigh between 2 to 3 pounds. They live in heavy timbered stands of mountainous country. Grouse roam widely to satisfy a varied diet which includes insects, berries, fruits, seeds and leaf buds.

They are noted for their exotic courtships. The male enacts a dignified performance and produces an exceptional call to lure nearby females into his harem. A cock will fluff out his feathers to increase the appearance of his size. With an erected chest, tail fanned and head held high, he'll strut around the female candidate.

He will suddenly stop and begin to beat the air with his wings until they are nothing more than a blur. The flapping of the wings produces a ''rolling boom sound'' like the deep muffled beating of a drum. The resounding love song can be heard for miles and is designed to attract any female within hearing distance.

The females alone are responsible for the nesting duties and rearing the young. A nest is built in the foot of a stump or log. Ten to fifteen eggs will be deposited and hatch in four weeks.

The young chicks will follow their mother around during the day in search of food. They will gather under the shelter of their mother's wings at night. They move up into tree roosts as soon as they can fly.

Grouse are superbly camouflaged. They use this camouflage to their advantage when hunted. They are capable of moving swiftly through the underbrush unseen.

If they are pressured, grouse will break from cover with a sudden burst of speed and noise that has caused many a startled hunter to drop his gun. Strong chest muscles allow for fast, controlled flights. The birds will endeavor to place as many trees between themselves and the hunter as quickly as possible.

REGULATIONS

The grouse season starts in mid-September and runs through November. You are allowed to take three birds in most of the units. There are no special license requirements to hunt grouse. All you need is a small game license.

HOW TO HUNT GROUSE

Blue grouse are high mountain birds. The first rule to remember when you hunt grouse is that they migrate up into the higher elevations in the fall and winter. Grouse live in the thick brush around creek bottoms in the summer. When the late summer heat dries out the berries, They begin to migrate up into the mountains.

They will continue their upward migration in pursuit of food until the first snowfall. At that point, the birds move up to the ridge lines where they will stay until the end of winter.

The best place to find grouse are in draws bordered on both sides by heavy timber. If you can find a draw that is covered with lots of low vegetation and grass, so much the better.

Draws are popular fall and winter feeding grounds for grouse. The inside of the draw is protected from adverse weather and therefore holds a better food supply. Draws also protect the birds from the wind which they do not like.

Once you find a suitable area, walk up the draw and follow it to the top. Resist the easier temptation to drive to the top of a draw and walking downhill.

Grouse will seldom fly uphill. If you ''walk up on them'', they will hold tight and flush when you are close enough for a shot. If you ''walk down on them'', they will flush and fly downhill well out of range of your shotgun.

As you move up the draw, scout the trees along the borders. Grouse move back and forth from the trees to the vegetation to feed. You can also find blue grouse walking along graveled mountain roads. They need gravel to supplement their digestive systems.

WHERE TO HUNT GROUSE

You can find good blue grouse hunting just about anywhere in the state where the elevation is above 8,000 feet with high stands of timber. The Top Flats Wilderness area is a good place to start. It supports the perfect grouse habitat including draws at a variety of elevations.

There is good public access into the Top Flats. To get there, take interstate 70 west from Denver. Exit on state 131 and go north to Yampa. Top Flats is west of Yampa in Dunkey Pass.

Trappers Lake southwest of Yampa is another good spot to try. The Marvin Lakes are in the Trapper Lake region and offer good grouse hunting. There are several trail heads that start at Marvin Lake.

The South Fork of the White River is a good grouse area. There are public camp sites at the South Fork Campground which you can use as your base camp. Hunt the trail heads and draws out of South Fork.

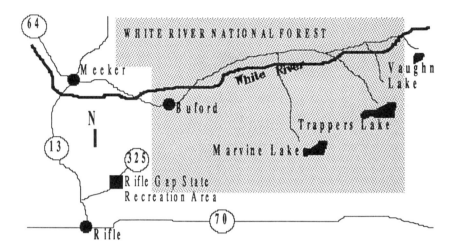

The southwest San Juan Mountains are one of the more consistent grouse hunting areas in the state. The terrain in the San Juan's are rugged which is why it's good grouse country. You have got to be in shape to hunt there.

The Weminuche Wilderness area is just below the San Juans and offers good grouse hunting. Try the draws along Vallecito Creek and the Florida River.

The Uncompahgre National Forest on the west side of the state has plenty of good grouse habitat. The area is covered with canyons and draws that hold the kind of vegetation grouse love.

The Red Feathers area in northeast Colorado supports some of the finest grouse hunting in the state. Try the draws in the Seven-Mile area along Swamp Creek, Pine Creek and George Creek.

All of the area east of Gunnison between Spring Creek and Taylor Park is good. There are a lot of grouse in the Granite Mountain and White Pines regions.

The Indian Peaks Wilderness area which is located 35 miles west of Boulder is another excellent blue grouse sanctuary. With over 70,000 public acres to hunt, you should have plenty of room to hunt.

PHEASANTS

The Chinese Ring-necked Pheasant was introduced into North America by the English in 1880. Pheasants now range throughout the New England and Middle Atlantic States, Midwest and the Pacific Northwest states.

A male pheasant will measure 33 inches long and weighs between 3 to 4 pounds. The head of the bird is green with a rich patch of red around the eye. The white ring at the base of the neck is where the nickname ''ring-neck'' comes from.

Pheasants nest in ground hallows lined with leaves, grass or straw. They prefer to nest in bushy pastures, grass or grain fields. The female will lay between 8 and 14 olive colored eggs. Only hours after the hatch, the new chicks are fully capable of running after their mother. Pheasants feed on corn, wheat, barley, wild fruits and insects.

The pheasant has short, broad wings which allow it to take off quickly into a steep climb when startled. They have become one of the more popular game birds in Colorado and are widely considered a delicacy.

REGULATIONS

The pheasant season starts in mid-October and runs through mid-January. You are allowed to take three (3) roosters per day. State game restrictions vary by region and zone. Consult the current regulations before you plan your hunt.

HOW TO HUNT PHEASANTS

Dedication is the key to becoming a sucessful pheasant hunter. Most of the birds will hide along the fringes of fields and river bottoms in the early season.

They will begin to move into thick cover as soon as there is snow. You'll find them in masses of brush at the edge of grain fields or in the brush along ravines.

When you find a good spot, hunt against the wind if possible. Pheasants tend to rise away from a hunter but will almost always turn to ride the wind. This will give you a better chance of getting a shot.

Fences lined with cover are good areas to walk. The birds can't move to the sides without being seen. They are more likely to stay in their place until you flush them.

Move slowly when you are stalking pheasants. Pheasants are experts at hiding and if given half a chance, they'll let you walk right by them. This is especially true late in the season when the birds have discovered hiding is an effective means of escape.

Vary your pace and stop every once in awhile. This tactic may convince a hidden bird that you have spotted it. He may flush while you are in a still position.

Also, change the way you walk if you don't have a dog. Make a mental map of the field or area that you plan to hunt. Plan out a walking course that will move the birds out into the open. Cover the best spots as you walk.

Hunt in a "zig-zaging" pattern as you walk. If you're hunting with a partner, "zig-zag" together in parallel patterns. If you are hunting with a dog, you don't have to do this.

A good dog will have been trained to "zig-zag" for you. A hunter with a trained pheasant dog will do ten times better than a hunter without one. Dogs can locate nine out of the ten pheasants that a hunter without a dog will never see.

Alternate your "stops and starts" with your partner. Hidden pheasants will try to keep track of both hunters and dogs if present. If one stops while the other keeps coming, they'll get nervous and are more apt to break cover. That is the whole idea of the game.

Hunt the brush along the edges of fields first. If there is corn stubble near by, look for the birds to flush and fly into the easier to hunt stubble. If they do, go in after them. Station one or more hunters out ahead of the area where they landed and then start "zig-zagging" in after them.

WHERE TO HUNT PHEASANTS

Northeast Colorado holds the prime pheasant country. The second best spot is located in the southeast corner of the state followed by the Colorado/Kansas border sections. There are a few spotted areas to hunt in the western half of the state.

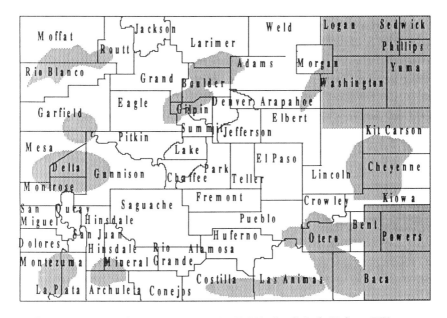

TOP PHEASANT HUNTING SPOTS

The prime northeast pheasant areas run from Fort Morgan to the Kansas, Nebraska borders. The Bob Elliot SWA is one of the more popular public areas to hunt. It's located east of Brush off U.S. 6.

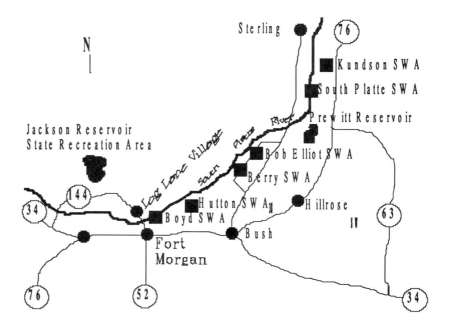

The Tamarack Ranch SWA is another good spot. The south Platte River winds through this fine property which is bordered by crop lands. All of this adds up to excellent pheasant country. Tamarack is located just off I-76.

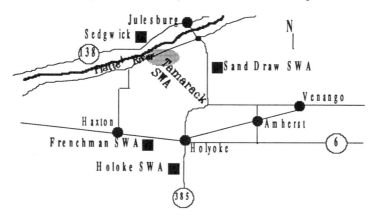

The South Republican SWA is considered by many hunters to be the top pheasant spot in the state. One reason is because it's next to the Kansas border which is full of pheasants. Hunt right along the edges of the Republican River and below the Bonny Reservoir dam.

The southeast part of the state offers some good hunting at Twin Buttes Reservoir SWA. The hunting is good from here all the way to the Kansas border.

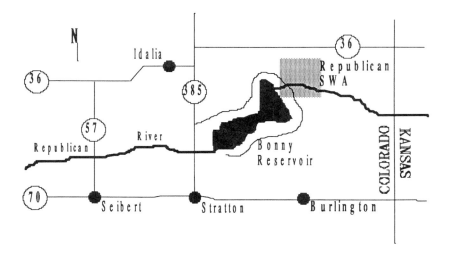

Other good southeastern areas include the west end of John Martin Reservoir near the inlet of the Arkansas River and Queens SWA. There is good hunting in the Arkansas Valley between Las Animas and Manzanola.

There is some decent pheasant hunting on the Western Slope. Escalante and Island Acres state wildlife areas are two spots to check out. Both get a lot of pressure. There is some BLM land that can be hunted along the Uncompahgre River east of Delta.

The Escalante SWA has some excellent pheasant habitat. The area is brushy with lots of ravines. As an added bonus, it is bordered by 700 acres of corn fields.

SAGE CHICKENS

The sage grouse or sage chicken as it is often called is one of the most exciting upland game birds to hunt. They are found in abundance in northern and southern Colorado and are particularly fond of the sage brush covered prairie regions of the western states.

Sage grouse are about 18 inches in length and will weigh between 2 and 3 pounds. They're sagebrush grey in color with a scattering of white spots to augment their superb camouflage characteristics.

The males are noted for the dignified performance which they put on during the courtship and mating season. Cocks will start their ritual in a prairie field by first fluffing out their feathers to appear twice their normal size.

If they are successful, they'll soon be surrounded by a flock of admiring hens. The cocks next move will be to raise his neck frills, puff out his chest, fan out his tail and with dragging wings, strut through the hens.

All of this is done to get the attention of the hens. If all else fails, he'll resort to beating his chest with a rapid flapping of wings to produce a sound similar to a muffled drum.

Once the mating season is over, the females take full charge of the nesting duties and the rearing of the young. A nest is prepared at the base of a clump of sage brush. Ten to fifteen eggs are deposited. They will hatch in four weeks.

After the "hatch", the chicks will wander out as a group to search for food in a manner similar to young domestic chickens. They remain with their mother until they reach full maturity.

Sage chickens are popular game birds in the rocky mountain states. However, their popularity in Colorado is somewhat less popular than what you'll find in states like Wyoming and Montana. That of course is good news for Colorado hunters who prefer to keep this hunting to themselves.

Properly prepared and cooked, sage chicken is really a "Western Gourmets Delight." There is nothing quite like it! Young birds, lightly floured and salted, cut up and fried in very hot deep oil (not too well done) is so good that even you will want to lock the doors to keep the neighbors out. Old birds are too tough to fry but make excellent stews. That's when you invite the neighbors in.

REGULATIONS

The sage chicken season starts in mid-September and runs through the first week of October. At this time, the young chickens hatched in the spring are suitable for the frying pan. If possible, try to avoid shooting the older birds which are only suitable for stews.

You're allowed to take three birds in most of the units. Most of the birds are downed with standard shotguns using 6 to 8 shot. There are no special license requirements to hunt sage chicken. All you need is a small game license.

HOW TO HUNT SAGE CHICKENS

At the first sight or sound of danger, these birds will sneak off quickly through the sage brush and will disappear into cover. You will literally have to walk over the top of them before they will flush. Their strong breast muscles enable them to suddenly burst from cover with a sufficient amount of noise that has caused many a startled hunter to drop his gun before he can shoot. They'll fly low over the brush to put as much brush between them and a hunter's gun.

If the weather is dry when you start your hunt, you'll find the birds clustered around water areas. A big Colorado rain storm will scatter the birds.

Start off your early morning hunt by scouting for birds in the grassy areas near the water. Prairie chickens will start to move toward the sage brush as soon as the sun comes up. By mid-day, they will all be out in the brush.

If you're in an area that allows you to scout above a creek, pond or lake, try using your binoculars to spot birds at the edge of the water when the sun comes up. Then, plan your stalk to where you have spotted the birds.

If you can find water adjacent to a grassy field, bordered by sage brush, you will have found the perfect sage chicken habitat. Hunt by walking along the border were the field joins the sage brush.

A dog will definitely improve your odds but, it is not a critical factor. If you jump sage chickens, they typically fly only a short distance which will give you a chance to find them again, without a dog.

However, there is no substitute for using a trained dog to retrieve a downed or wounded bird. If you wound one of these birds, move quickly to locate your bird. A wounded bird can cover a lot of ground on foot and at a pace that will challenge the best of dogs.

Here are a couple of hints on shooting techniques. Sage chicken are slow at take off. They will hover for an instance when they start their vertical take off above the brush, before they shoot forward over the top of the brush. If you're "quick on the draw," your best shot will happen during the vertical take off phase.

WHERE TO HUNT SAGE CHICKENS

The three "hot spot" regions in the state are in the northwest corner of the state, Gunnison Basin and North Park. All support a good population of birds.

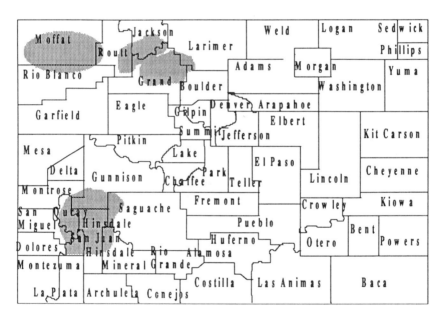

TOP SAGE CHICKEN HUNTING SPOTS ▨

The Blue Mountain area near the Utah border is one of the better areas. There is plenty of public land in the Rangly area, which is located a few miles south of Blue Mountain.

Next, try the area directly north of Maybell. There are many prime agricultural fields which border the sage brush. If you can obtain access permission to private land, you should have no problems finding birds.

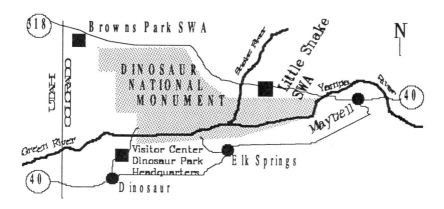

If you drive directly west of Craig to Juniper Springs, you should find birds. The other alternative is to take County Road 7 out of Craig and head west to The Great Divide. The area north of Craig between County Road 101 and Highway 13 supports a good population of birds. One of the better areas to hunt is along the Fortification Creek drainage.

The Routt National Forest on either side of Yampa is a good area to hunt, and it typically gets very little pressure. The Green Ridge, Hunt Creek and Oak Creek areas are all good.

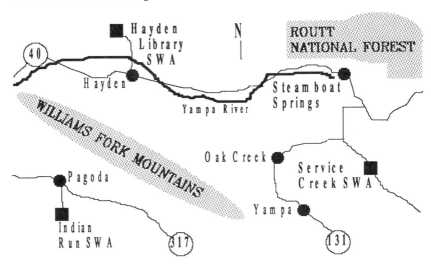

The Gunnison Basin to the south can offer some outstanding hunting opportunities. Try the area along the Taylor River north of Gunnison. You should also be able to find birds east of town along highway 50.

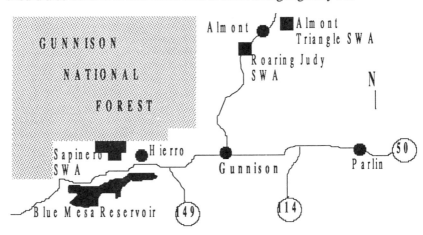

There is an area called north and south Parlin Flats located just outside of Parlin, Colorado that deserves mention. In this area, there are a lot of good river bottoms to hunt which are bordered by sage brush.

Dinner on the Run . . **COUGAR-WHITETAIL**   ©1978 by Bill O'Neill   p.o. box 1333, livingston, montana 59047 Ph. (406) 587-9460

CHAPTER 10

VARMINT HUNTING

COYOTES

Coyotes are a relatively small animals. They will measure about 2 feet at the shoulder and weigh between 40 and 60 pounds. They are reddish gray in color with an extended bushy black tipped tail.

Coyotes can be found hunting any time of the day, but are more active at dusk and at night. They'll eat what ever they can catch including rabbits, all types of rodents, gophers, birds, snakes, lizards, frogs, and insects.

They will frequently hunt in pairs or groups of three or four. Coyotes have been known to take larger prey such as deer and antelope by working together in packs. A common tactic is for a single dog to chase prey into a waiting ambush from the pack.

Well adapted to a variety of habitat, they can run for extended periods at speeds up to 40 mph. They're fully capable of covering a territory of 400 miles in a week. Coyotes will "turn" vegetarian if they can not find prey animals.

It is believed that coyotes mate for life. Mating season occurs from February through April. Litters of 8 to 12 pups are common. The young are usually born in a den at the end of a cave.

REGULATIONS

You are required to have a small game licence if you intend to hunt coyotes. The season is open all year. Coyote "furs" can be sold to a furrier in the winter months. Winter pelt prices will vary anywhere from $30 to $75 per pelt, depending upon fur condition and color.

HOW TO HUNT COYOTES

The most popular way to hunt coyotes is with a call that sounds like a wounded rabbit. You are allowed to use either mouth or taped cassette calls. As a general rule, the higher-pitched calls work best. You can change the pitch of mouth calls by controlling the airflow going through the call.

When you first start calling for coyotes, use a light modified call to get their attention. Most coyotes will come loping straight toward a call until he feels he's close enough to start stalking. In most cases, that will happen when he's between 100 and 200 yards of the caller.

WHERE TO HUNT COYOTES

Coyote hunting in Colorado is good anywhere. It all depends upon your preference for hunting style and the quality of the pelt you're after. There are hunters who like to hunt on cross country skis. They'll head up into North Park and Moffat Counties to find the best pelts.

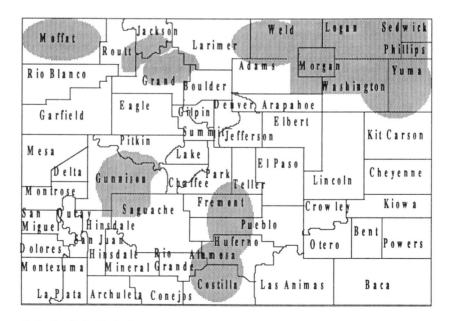

TOP COYOTE HUNTING SPOTS ■

Most of the successful hunting is done at the lower elevations. There are a lot of dogs all over the eastern plains. The trick is to find an area that hasn't already had a great deal of hunting pressure and supports plenty of coyote food such as rabbits.   Yuma County is one of the most popular coyote hunting counties. The South Platte Valley always seems to deliver a high number of dogs.

The northeast part of the state offers   excellent coyote hunting in the Pawnee National Grasslands.   The grasslands are a large patchwork of national forest land. You'll need a map to effectively hunt the area. Contact the Forest Service office in Greeley.

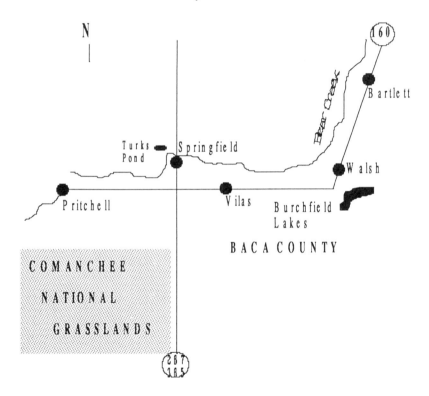

Further south, hunters will find good hunting throughout the Arkansas Valley. The best areas to concentrate on are in the Pueblo, Crowley and the Otero River bottoms.   Another alternative is to drive south into Baca County and eastern Las Animas counties. The Camanche Grasslands provide a lot of coyote hunting area. Hunt the canyons for best results.

Some of the best hunting in the state is in Huerfano County. This is where the pros work, so it gets professional pressure. The Sage Flats area south of Gunnison offer excellent hunting. Most of this is BLM land so access isn't a problem. Hunt the area south of Cooper Mountain Road or Cochetopa Creek.

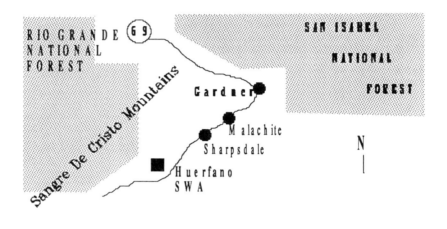

Another good area to hunt is Montezuma Valley near Cortez. To the north is the Paradox Valley on the west side of the Uncompahgre Plateau. On the other side of the plateau, hunters will find lots of coyotes in the Uncompahgre Valley.

PRAIRIE DOGS

The prairie dog is one of the larger ground squirrels. They will measure about a foot in length and weigh up to 3 pounds. Their range extends from the extreme portions of south central Canada through the Rocky Mountain, midwest and southwest states and on into Mexico.

One of the more gregarious of animals, the prairie dog constructs extensive and elaborate networks of tunnels and burrows, with underground chambers throughout their prairie habitat. These animals live in "prairie dog towns" which may include burrows covering several hundreds of acres and a population of several thousands of prairie dogs.

Towns are divided into smaller territories called "wards" which are made up of family groups called "coteries". One male, three to four females and their young form a coterie.

Prairie dogs will dig a burrow which will extent about four vertical feet below the surface before the tunnel turns laterally into extended hallways. Several nest and excrement chambers are built along the hallway. The burrows forming individual "wards" will be inter-linked to expand the underground colony.

The prairie dog covers its excrement with dirt. When the excrement chamber becomes filled with dirt, it is closed off and a new one is opened. Nesting chambers are lined with grass and excess fur.

The activity of the prairie dog is dependent upon the weather. On very hot days, the "dogs" will stay in their burrows to avoid the heat. They will come out to forage in the morning or late evening. On cool days, they'll be out all day. They feed on prairie grasses and insects. On occasion, they will eat meat.

The mating season runs through February and March. After a gestation period of one month, a litter of four to five young are born in a chamber. The young will emerge from the burrow when they are 6 weeks old. They will be on their own in 10 weeks.

The prairie dog population increased sharply after the buffalo was almost eliminated at the turn of the century. They became formidable competitors with cattle for prairie grasses. Ranchers embarked on extensive campaigns with poisons to eliminate prairie dogs.

More recent wildlife studies indicate that balanced populations of prairie dog colonies help to propagate the natural underground irrigation system of the prairie.

REGULATIONS

The hunting season for prairie dogs is year-around in Colorado. You are required to have a small game license to hunt these animals. There are no daily limits on the number of animals which you may take.

HOW TO HUNT PRAIRIE DOGS

Prairie dogs are the single most popular varmint animal to hunt in Colorado. A hunter can easily "burn up" in excess of several hundred rounds of ammo in a single day hunting these crafty animals.

Many state ranchers consider excess populations of prairie dogs an unwanted pest. Permission to hunt private land is relatively easy to obtain. A good rifle with a 10 to 12 power scope are a prerequisite if you plan to hunt prairie dogs. The popular varmint gun calibers include the .220 Swift, .222 and .223 Rimington.

Your gun should be sighted in to "hit a fly" at 300 yards. Tripods are often used to help improve the accuracy of long range shots. Spotting scopes are another added convenience to help locate "dog towns".

Prairie dog activity increases as the weather warms up. In the early spring, the dogs are most active during the midday. When the hot weather moves in with the summer months, they'll come out in the mornings and evenings and stay in their burrows at midday to avoid the heat.

Prairie dogs will run for cover if they see anything that moves. These animals are extremely sensitive to protecting themselves from predators and human hunters are on the top of their list.

You will have better luck if you hunt on a clear day. Hawks and eagles are one of the prairie dog's biggest natural enemies. On a clear day, they can see the shadows of the big birds on the ground which is their "early warning system." On cloudy days, they can't see shadows and tend to be more nervous.

WHERE TO HUNT PRAIRIE DOGS

There are a significant number of prairie dog colonies all along the Front Range. The Pawnee National Grasslands in northeast Colorado offer some top shooting on public land.

There are some prairie dogs east of Greely along the South Platte River and north of Denver along the Front Range. Most of the land here is private so you will need to get permission.

There is excellent hunting in the southeast part of the state. The Comanche Grasslands offer several thousand acres of fine public hunting.   There is good hunting just about anywhere between Colorado Springs and Pueblo. If you drive the country roads, you'll spot the towns.

The northwest part of the state offers good hunting around Grand Junction. There are some good size towns off Interstate 70. The Book Cliffs area is a good spot to try.

There is some BLM land west of the town of Mack that is worth trying. You will find most of the dogs to the north of Highline Canal and west of Highway 139.

The best hunting is in the southwest part of the state. The south Gunnison area along Highway 114 includes a mix of private and public land. The Cochetopa area is open to the public and is full of prairie dog towns. If you can get access to private land, try the Ohio Creek area north of Gunnison.

The are a lot of dogs to hunt in the Esclante State Wildlife Area which is located 5 miles west of Delta along Highway 50. This area gets a lot of pressure so the dogs tend to be very wary.

WINTER MALLARDS ©1975 by *Bill O'Neil* p.o.box 1333, livingston, mont. 590

CHAPTER 11

WATERFOWL

DUCKS

A variety of ducks inhabit Colorado including block, pintail, teal, canvas back, wood and mallards. The mallard is by far the most abundant and popular wild duck to hunt in the state.

Mallards are one of the largest of the "duck family." They will grow to a length of 18 inches. As is true with most ducks, there is a pronounced difference in the coloration of the sexes.

The males (drakes) have a bright green head with a white ring around the base of the neck. The body is greyish-brown and is supported by bright orange feet. The female (hen) is colored dusky-brown with a purple patch an each wing.

The color differences serve two basic purposes. The drakes use their colors to attract the hens. The hens use their colors to blend into their nesting sites.

Nests are constructed on the ground by the females. Hidden in vegetation, the hen builds an incubator of fine reeds, grass and leaves lined with soft down feathers which she supplies from her own body. Six to ten green-brown eggs are laid. They will hatch in 28 days.

Mallards have developed a wide ranging appetite which include frogs, tadpoles, lizards, newts, fish, snails, earthworms, insects, mice, grasses, seeds and aquatic plants.

They have been very successful at adapting to a wide variety of urban, simi-urban and wild habitats. This is the primary reason for their survival success.

REGULATIONS

The statewide season opens the first part of October and closes at mid-month.   It reopens again at the end of the month and closes the end of November.   The third and final season runs from mid-December to mid-January.

The typical bag limit is five birds.   There are a number of restrictions which apply to the bag limit depending upon where you hunt. Check the latest regulations carefully.

HOW TO HUNT DUCKS

Hunting ducks is most often thought of in term of a blind, decoys, calling and an eager retriever. This is of course one method, but there are others. Pass shooting is one, but it is very often a gamble with the odds in favor of the ducks who know how to fly well out of the range of your shotgun.

Another method is jump shooting. While this technique may not offer the assurance that you can expect from hiding in a blind with decoys, it is one of the more exciting ways to hunt ducks. There is nothing like having a bird spring up from nowhere, unexpectedly.

If you think you are into jump shooting, scout small rivers with still pools that wind through open meadows and pastures. Find a high spot such as a ridge line were you can climb above the river for stalking. Once you spot ducks, mark their location with some kind of landmark such as a tree and plan your stalk accordingly.

If you are right on when you sneak up on the ducks, they should flush as soon as you appear in their view. If you miss your mark, and they are downstream from where you thought they would be, they'll take off as soon as they see you.

Float trips down a river are another popular way to jump-shoot ducks. Anything that floats including canoes and rubber rafts will work. Look for ducks along the shoreline as you float through the loops of the river.

There are a host of safety factors to keep in mind when jump-shooting ducks from a floating platform. The excitement that can be generated when a bunch of ducks suddenly raised off the water has caused many a boat to tip over.   Icy water that flows with the fall and winter hunting months can be very debilitating. Flotation vest are a "must wear" for this type of hunting.

Although jump and pass shooting are very popular and quite effective, it becomes harder to hunt this way as the season progresses. Most of the birds have been shot at a number of time and have learned to select water sites out of range of any shotgun.

Decoy hunting can be very effective to lure wary birds to within range of your gun. Arrange decoys in either a ''V'' or ''J'' pattern. The tip of the ''V'' or the bottom of the ''J'' should be pointed toward your blind. The opening of your pattern should face the wind. The whole idea is to allow the birds to fly right into the decoys.

Place your decoys about 20 to 25 yards from the blind. Don't bunch up the decoys. Ducks tend to bunch together when they are nervous and if passing ducks sense this, they won't land. Also, landing birds like to drop into water where there is plenty of room.

Scout out possible areas to set your decoys. Watch the pattern of the birds as they take off and come into the area you plan to hunt. Set up your decoys accordingly.

The best shotgun to use is a 12-gauge with a modified choke. Most counties require the use of steel shot shells. Recommended shot size for steel is 2 or 4 shot (4 or 6 for lead).

WHERE TO HUNT DUCKS

The best duck hunting is generally found in the central and eastern half of the state. The exception is the Grand Junction area and the section along the Colorado River.

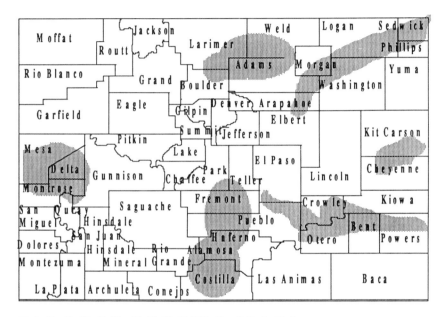

T O P   D U C K   H U N T I N G   S P O T S

The San Louis Valley and the Rio Grande are the most consistent spots to hunt ducks in the state. There are four top public areas starting with Monte Vista National Wildlife Refuge, Alamosa National Wildlife Area, the lower Arkansas River and the Rio Grande State Wildlife Area.

Duck hunting in any one of these areas can be excellent as long as the water in the marshes does not freeze. The most popular approach is to put on waders and wade out into the marsh. Set up your decoys, hide in the tules and wait for the ducks to come to you.

The best hunting along the Arkansas is on either side of Lamar. You'll find most of the birds holding up on the slow-moving stretches of the river. The ducks will move off the Arkansas at night to feed in the near-by fields. At first morning light, they'll fly along the river looking for a place to land. The use of decoys on the river can be very effective.

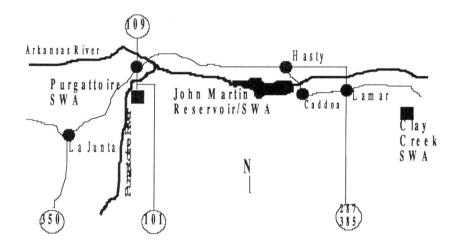

There is also good hunting in Jackson County which is north of San Luis Valley. The early season hunts are good at Lake John, Crowdrey, Delaney Butte and all the other lakes in the county.

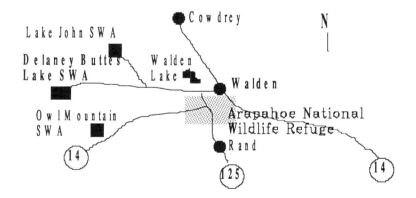

The birds move out of the lakes as the season matures and they wise up to "what's going on." They will fan out into the rivers and streams. The ducks fly up and down the waterways offering hunters excellent pass shooting.

The Pawnee Grasslands in the northeast part of the state offers good hunting in the early season. There are lots of pond-size pot holes in the Grasslands that attract ducks until they freeze over.

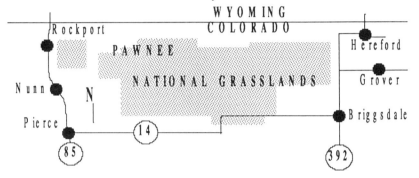

The Wellington SWA is another good area to hunt in the northeast. It's located just north of Fort Collins off I-25. The best time to hunt this marshy area is after a couple of good fall storms have pushed the birds off the Front Range lakes.

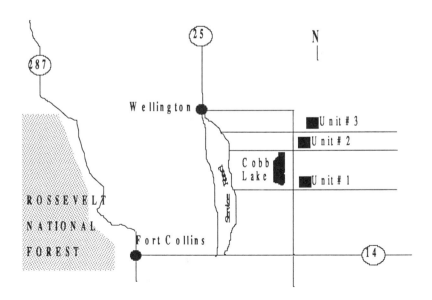

Shadow Mountain Reservoir over by Granby can be very good in the early season. Hunt along the shoreline with decoys. If you have a boat, take your decoys out to any one of the islands on the lake and set up your blind there.

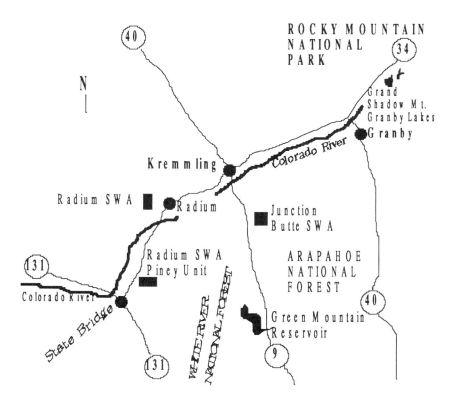

Lake Granby is right next to Shadow Mountain and can be hunted the same way. It's considerably larger than Shadow Mountain. The birds tend to be more scattered than they are on Shadow Mountain.

Northwest Colorado hunters can enjoy excellent jump shooting along the Yampa and White rivers. Steamboat Lake is in the same area and is probably the best duck hunting spot in the northwest.

The Steamboat Marina rents boats and decoys. The southwest corner of the lake along the shoreline seems to produce the most ducks. Pearl Lake is close by and also offers plenty of ducks.

One of the top lakes in the state is Bonney Reservoir. It's 200 miles east of Denver almost on the Kansas border. As many as 60,000 birds will move into Bonney before the season ends. As an added bonus, the Republican River flows into the bottom of the reservoir and offers some excellent jump shooting.

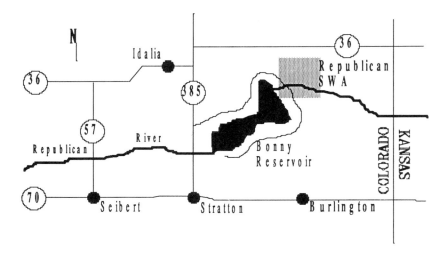

The best decoy hunting is along the north shoreline. The mouth of the Republican River is also a good area to set up decoys. If you spread out from the river, you'll run into plenty of small ponds that also hold lots of ducks. If the action slows down on the decoys, try jump shooting the ponds.

The South Platte River is one of the more consistent late season spots. The river runs from the Nebraska border all the way down to Brighton. The entire stretch is good. However, the closer you get to Denver, the heavier the pressure.

The Tamarack Ranch State Wildlife Area offers about 12 miles of public access to the Platte River between Julesburg and Sterling. It's located east of Sterling off I-76 and can be accessed by taking either Proctor, Cook or Red Lion Road exits.

There are 40 waterfowl units along the river which are available on a first come basis. The check station opens two hours before shooting time. Weekend pressure can get heavy. You can just about pick your spot durring the week.

GEESE

Canadian geese are by far the most predominant game birds to hunt in Colorado. These large black necked birds are migratory, and nest in the immense stretches of the Canadian marshes which extend almost to the Arctic coast. Geese also breed in many localities of northwestern United States and Colorado.

There are eleven subspecies of the Canadian goose. They all share the same coloring which starts with a long black neck, black head and white cheek patches under the neck. The body is brownish grey with a pale belly and black tail.

The main difference in the varying specie is size. The wing spread of the small Crackling Goose is 22 inches as compared to 48 inches for the Giant Canada Goose.

Each year, over 3,000,000 of these fabulous birds migrate over four age old routes known as flyways. The flyways are known as the Pacific, Atlantic, Mississippi and Central flyways.

Geese fly south out of Canada in the fall and return to their Canadian nesting grounds in the spring. Each flyway has national wildlife refuges well spaced along the way to offer the birds safety and food.

An internal biological clock and navigational system guides the geese durring their migration cycle. Scientists believe that these birds navigate by using an inborn star chart.

Geese travel in family groups and are typically seen flying in "V" formations. They will fly as high as 9,000 feet. A lead bird forms the point of the "V" to break up the air for the other birds in the formation.   The forward bird is not necessarily the group leader. Different birds will rotate in and out of this position to relieve the lead bird.

Geese feed on aquatic plants which they yank up from the bottoms of ponds with their beaks. The water is strained through a row of teeth like surfaces which line the inside of the beak. This also allows the birds to strip kernels of corn from a cob or clip grass when they are eating in open fields.

The mating season starts in the winter. Geese select partners for life at this time.   Mates are fiercely loyal to each other. They also prefer to intermingle only with members of their family.

Nesting sites are chosen in areas where their is isolation, good visibility, and nearby browsing. The nest is constructed of grass and twigs and lined with down which the birds pull from their breasts.   Four to five eggs are laid in early June. They'll hatch in 28 to 30 days. The young are able to swim with their parents within 24 hours after the hatch. They are able to fly in 45 to 60 days.

REGULATION

The statewide season opens the first part of October and closes at mid-month. It reopens again at the end of October and closes the end of November. The third and final season runs from mid-December to mid-January.

The typical bag limit is five birds. However, there are a number of local restrictions which may apply depending upon where you hunt. Check the latest regulations carefully.

HOW TO HUNT GEESE

Stalking is one popular way to hunt geese. To set up your stalk, drive to an open body of water where you are allowed to hunt. Use your binoculars to locate a flock of geese which can usually be found in the middle of the lake. Early morning is generally the best time to find geese this way. They'll be getting ready to leave the open water for their favorite feeding field.

As the geese leave the lake, remember their flight pattern and watch where they go. Return to the lake the next morning just before sunrise. Position yourself in the path that the geese will take when they leave. Set out as many decoys as you can and prepare a blind. You can use the same technique to hunt returning geese in the evening.

If there is snow on the ground, you can use a white sheet to conceal yourself. If the ground is bare, use tan colored camouflage covering to do the trick.

Your blind should be set up along the edge of the lake where you saw the geese fly over the evening before. Geese are creatures of habit. Chances are they will return to the same spot on the lake, entering the same way they took off.

Stay put until they get to within range which can be nerve wracking. Geese will often circle a sight several times before they make their final decent. As the season progresses, the migrating birds will join the locals. This adds to the action. A blind is a requisite if you plan to hunt in an open field. Pit blinds are the best but usually exist only on private lands.

WHERE TO HUNT GEESE

The best goose hunting is in the north central part of the state along the Interstate 25 corridor. The Grand Junction area along the Colorado river is a close second.

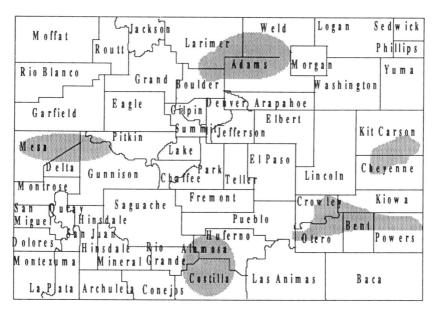

T O P   G O O S E   H U N T I N G   S P O T S

Boulder and Weld counties are considered the best goose hunting counties in the state. Anywhere from 80,000 to 120,000 birds will winter in these two counties alone. However, finding a place to hunt can be a real challenge.

Boulder Reservoir, Barbour Ponds and Boyd Lake offer three good public hunting alternatives. The best shooting is in and around the corn, alfalfa and grain fields. In the early morning, the birds fly off the water to the fields to feed. They'll return to the water in the evening. Most of the hunting here is pass shooting.

The best pass shooting at Boulder Reservoir is on the dam or next to the spill-way on the northwest side of the lake. There are also some pass shooting opportunities at Valmont Lake.

   Some of the best shooting in the state occurs along the South Platte River
east of Greeley. The top lakes in the area include Riverside, Empire and
Jackson Lake. Windsor Reservoir is west of Greeley and always supports a
large population of birds.

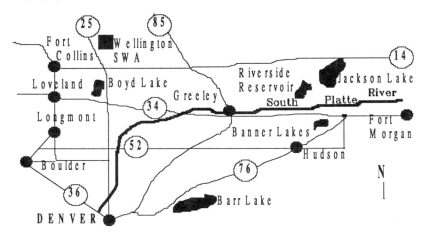

   Jackson Lake is open to public hunting on the north and west sides of the
lake. The area improves later in the season when the northern geese move into
the state.
   The Wellington State Wildlife Area offers find goose hunting fifteen
miles northeast of Fort Collins. This 2,300 acre park is bordered by cornfields
which attract the geese like a magnet.   Barr Lake State Park is another good
public hunting area. The park is located 8 miles east of Brighton. There are
14 blinds available on a lottery basis.

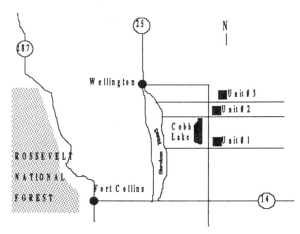

The Republican State Wildlife Area offers good shooting opportunities for geese that come off Bonney Reservoir in the morning. They will return from the Kansas grain fields in the evening which makes the area excellent for pass shooting. The area is located 200 miles east of Denver.

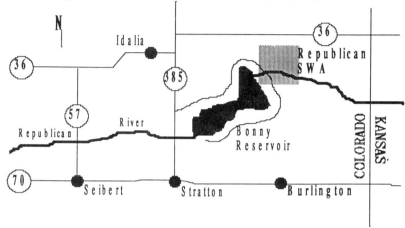

One of the best areas in the state is the Arkansas River Valley. As many as 20,000 geese will move into the area by the end of the season. The best hunting is in the grain fields bordering the reservoirs along the Arkansas River.

There is good public hunting access at Queens State Wildlife Area. It's located 5 miles west of Lamar on U.S. 50. There are 7,200 acres of water and 1,900 acres of land to hunt so you should have plenty of "elbow room."

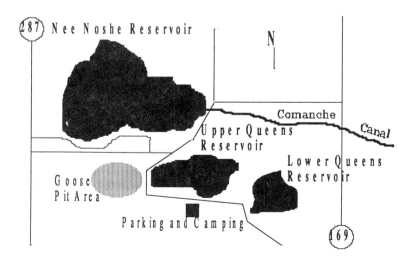

There are several ways to hunt Queens. You can field shoot from pit blinds with decoys. Pass shooters can shoot from blinds or simply hide in a cluster of sage brush. There are about 30 blinds available to hunters on a "first come, first serve" basis.

The goose pit blinds are located between the Upper Queens and the Nee Noshe Reservoirs. If you are unable to get a blind, try the firing line on the south side of Nee Noshe Reservoir.

The western slope is typically thought of as "the place you go to hunt big game." However, it does offer some good waterfowl hunting. Most of the hunting is done off the numerous stretches of rivers located in the area.

The exception is Sweitzer Lake State Recreation Area. It's located just off the Gunnison River southeast of Delta. You must apply for a permit to hunt this area. There is also good hunting along the Uncompahgre River.

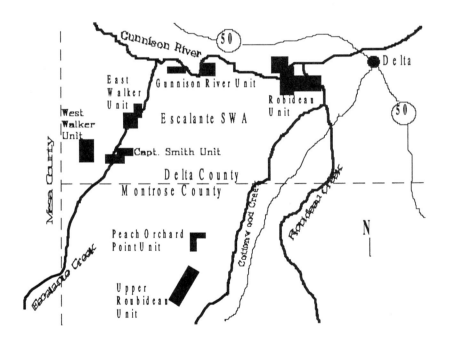

Highline State Recreation Area is open to hunters during the week. It's located 6 miles north of Loma on Highway 139. The north end of Highline Lake is the best area to hunt.

Escalante is another good SWA to hunt. There are five acres of ponds and five miles of supporting streams in the area to attract the geese. The total area covers 7,500 acres so you will have lots of room to hunt. Escalante SWA is 5 miles west of Delta

Royal Duel (elk) p.o. box 1333, livingston, montana 59047 Ph. (406) 587-9460

CHAPTER 12

PUBLIC HUNTING AREAS

Colorado owns and leases thousands of acres which are reserved for State Wildlife Areas or "SWA" in the abbreviated form. It is one of the finest public land access programs found anywhere in the country. In this chapter, we have listed the State's counties in alphabetical order and cover the SWAs in each county. We have also included a state map to help you locate a particular county you might want to hunt.

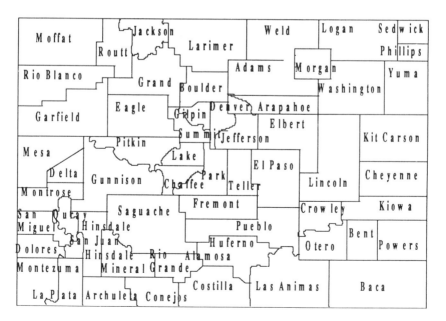

COUNTY DIRECTORY TO CHAPTER 12

ALAMOSA COUNTY

San Louis Lake SWA is located 13 miles north of Alamosa on Highway 17. The area is made up of 2,054 acres of land and 315 acres of lakes. It offers hunting opportunities for small game and waterfowl.

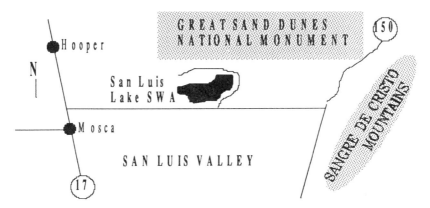

ARCHULETA COUNTY

Devil Creek SWA is located 16 miles west of Pogosa Springs off Highway 160. It includes 561 acres of land and 9 acres of streams and beaver dams. Big game and upland game hunting are permitted in the park which also includes camping facilities.

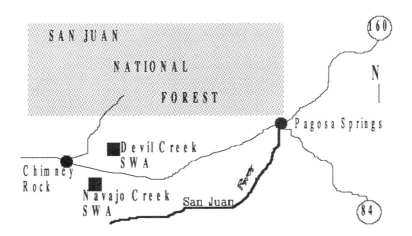

Navajo SWA is 13 miles west of Pagosa Springs on Highway 160. It is adjacent to the Navajo State Recreation Area which has camping and boat launch facilities. The area covers 520 acres of land plus the 1,500 acre Navajo Reservoir. Big and small game plus waterfowl hunting are all part of Navajo.

BUCA COUNTY

Burchfield Lake is 11 miles east of Walsh on Highway 116. It's made up of 177 acres of land and some small lakes. There are camping facilities on the property and small game hunting is allowed.

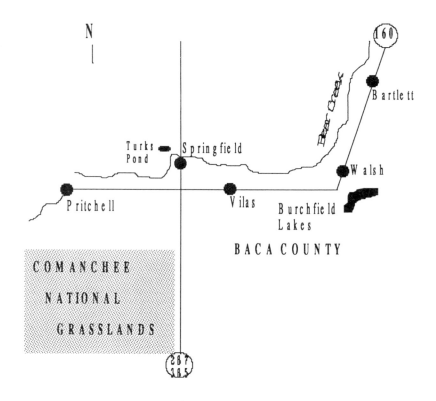

Turks Pond is a 200 acre SWA 2 miles north of Springfield off Highway 287. There are 39 acres of ponds on the property. Small game and waterfowl hunting are permitted.

Two Buttes Reservoir is located in the southeast corner of the state. Two Buttes is also one of the most under used parks in the state. It's located 36 miles south of Lamar off U.S. 287 and offers a variety of hunting and recreational opportunities. All of the state's game birds, small game and mule deer inhabit this 4,962 acre park.

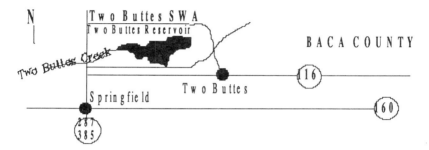

BENT COUNTY

Adobe Creek Reservoir offers excellent waterfowl hunting on over 5,000 acres of water. Camping facilities include toilets and a boat launch area. Adobe Creek is located 10 miles east of Arlington.

Horse Creek Reservoir is 18 miles north of La Junta off Highway 109. This 2,500 acre SWA offers both waterfowl and small game hunting opportunities.

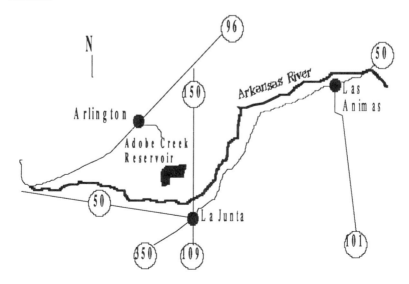

John Martin Reservoir is one of the largest SWAs in the state. It includes over 20,000 acres of land and 1,700 acres of water. John Martin is located 20 miles east of Las Animas and 25 miles west of Lamar off U.S. 50. It offers excellent duck and goose hunting. The state has installed goose pits which are available to hunter on a first come, first serve basis.

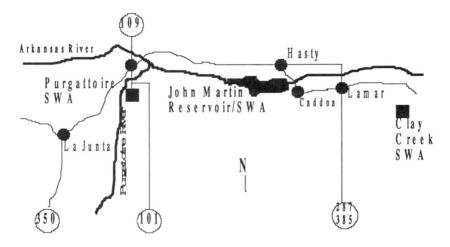

Las Animas SWA is 2 miles north of Las Animas and includes 38 acres of land. Waterfowl and small game hunting are allowed on the property. Purgatoire River is 2 miles south of Las Animas and features waterfowl and upland game bird hunting. This 960 acre SWA includes 1 mile of Purgatoire River frontage open to public hunting.

CHAFFEE COUNTY

Chaffee Creek is 13 miles north of Buena Vista off Highway 24. This 350 acre SWA includes the 150 acre Chaffee Reservoir. Big game and waterfowl hunting are popular at Chaffee. There are camping and boat launch facilities in the park.

CUSTER COUNTY

Middle Taylor Creek is made up of 486 acres of land and small creeks. It's located 8 miles west of Westcliff on the Hermit Lakes Road. The area offers both small and big game hunting with camping facilities.

DELTA COUNTY

McCluskey Easement SWA is 5 miles southwest of Paonia. There are 1,600 acres of land in the park which supports big and small game hunting. Roeber SWA is 4 miles southeast of Paonia. It covers 1,030 acres of land and is popular for big game hunting. There are some primitive camp sites in the area.

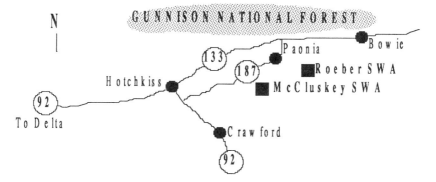

The Escalante SWA is made up of 7,500 acres of land which ranges from river bottom land to sage brush and pinion juniper forest. The park is located 13 miles west of Delta off Highway 50. It supports just about every game animal in the state including deer, elk, antelope, turkeys, waterfowl quail, pheasants, rabbits and band-tailed pigeons.

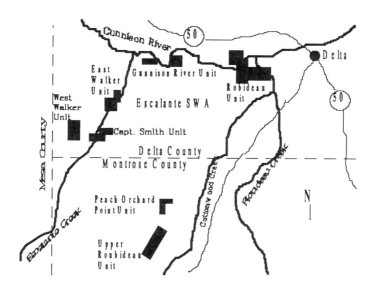

DELORES COUNTY

The Delores River SWA is 26 miles northwest of Cortez, off Highway 666. The area is made up of 1,220 acres of land, streams and ponds. Big and small game hunting are allowed in the area.

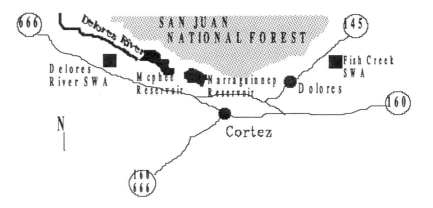

The Fish Creek SWA is 25 miles south of Norwood off Highway 145. There are 309 acres of land and about one mile of streams in the area. Big game and upland game bird hunting is popular on the property.

The Lone Cone SWA includes 5,000 acres of land and is next to Dry Creek SWA which adds another 8,000 acres to the area. There are another 17,000 acres of BLM land adjacent to the parks. The areas are all popular with big game hunters. There are primitive camping facilities on the properties. Lone Cone is located 2 miles east of Norwood on Highway 145. Dry Creek is 17 miles southeast of Norwood off Highway 141.

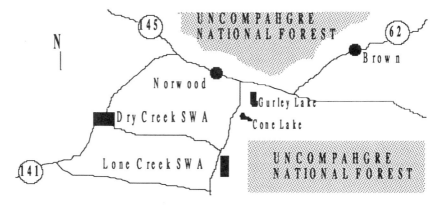

EAGLE COUNTY

Basalt SWA covers 528 acres of land. It's located 5 miles east of Basalt. The park supports big game hunting. Christine SWA is 1 mile west of Basalt on Highway 82 and includes 4,170 acres of land and some water. Camping sites are available at Christine.

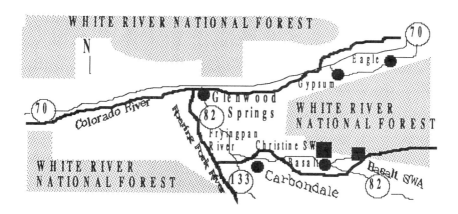

Dotsero SWA is 7 miles north of the town of Dotsero. There are 2,510 acres of land and small streams that are open to big game hunting. This park also   offers some excellent small game hunting. The small streams provide good habitat for duck and geese.

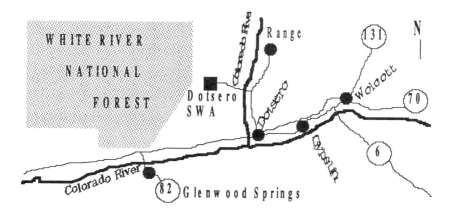

The Radium SWA consist of over 10,000 acres of some of the finest deer winter range in the state. The area also provides access to Bureau of Land Management land and national forest land. The park literally surrounds the town of Radium which is 20 miles southwest of Kremmling off Highway 131. Junction Butte SWA covers 1,300 acres of land south of Kremmling off State Highway 9. The park offers elk, deer and blue grouse.

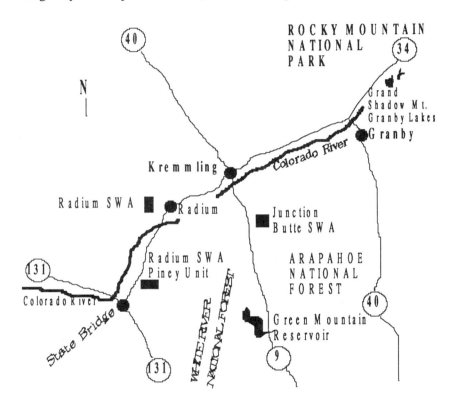

EL PASO COUNTY

The Colorado Springs SWA is a big 5,100 acre park that is just off I-25 between Colorado Springs and Pueblo. Although you are prohibited from using rifles and handguns on the property, shotguns and bows are allowed. There are several species of game birds to hunt including waterfowl, quail and dove.

GARFIELD COUNTY

Garfield Creek is located 1 mile southwest of New Castle on Highway 6. Exit south on county road 312 and follow the signs to the park's entrance. The park includes 4,800 acres of big and small game hunting.

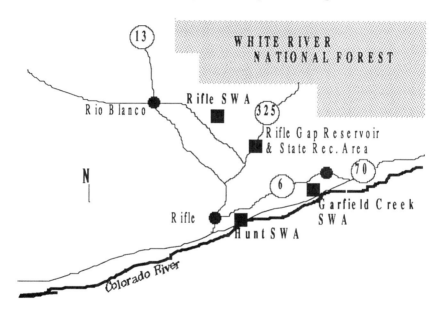

Rifle Creek SWA is 1 mile northwest of Rifle Gap Reservoir. It covers 320 acres of land and 2 miles of Rifle Creek frontage along with camping and toilet facilities. Big and small game hunting are allowed.

The 165 acre Hunt SWA supports good waterfowl hunting. The park is located 1 mile east of Rifle on the south side of the frontage road which runs parallel to Interstate 70.

GRAND COUNTY

Hot Sulfur Springs SWA is 2 miles west of the town of Hot Sulfur Springs on Highway 40. There is camping and toilets in the park which covers 1,775 acres of big game hunting terrain.

Junction Butte includes 1,300 acres of land northeast Radium and south of Kremmling off State Highway 9. The park offers elk, deer and blue grouse hunting.

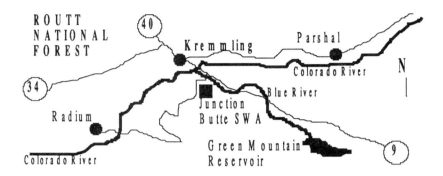

GUNNISON COUNTY

The Almont Triangle SWA is 3 miles north of the town of Almont on Highway 135. It covers 640 acres of big and small game hunting terrain. The Roaring Judy SWA literally surrounds Almont.

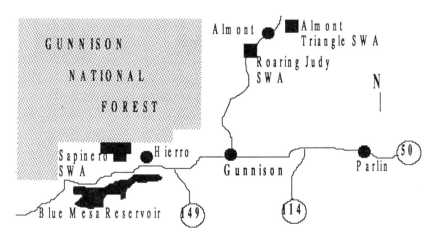

Sapinero SWA is one of the larger parks in the state covering over 7,000 acres of land. It's 15 miles west of Gunnison and 1 mile north of the Blue Mesa Reservoir. Sapinero is a popular area with big game hunters. There are camping facilities on the property.

HINSDALE COUNTY

Browns Lake is a 520 acre SWA located 22 miles west of Creede off Highway 149. Exit at the Hermit Lakes access road. The park offers both big and small game hunting.

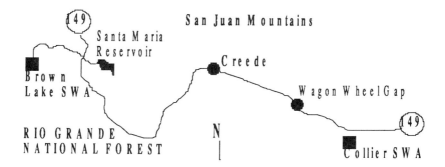

Cobolla Creek is a 1,430 acre park offering big game hunting. To get there, head west on Highway 50 out of Gunnison to Highway 149. Take 149 south and exit at Powderhorn. Follow the signs to the park. There are camping facilities on the property.

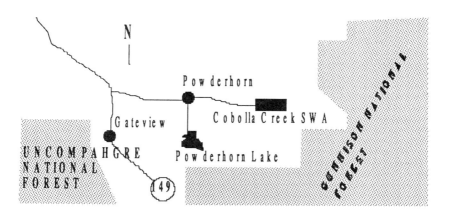

HUERFANO COUNTY

The Huerfano SWA is 13 miles southwest of Gardner and covers 545 acres of land. There is both big and small game hunting on the property.

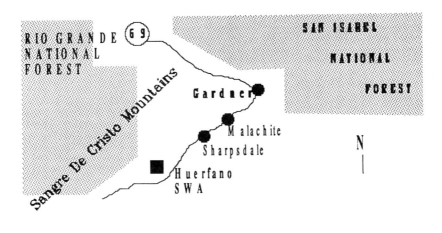

Wahatoya SWA is 1 mile east of La Veta on the Bear Creek Road. There are 160 acres of land and 45 acres of water on the property which supports waterfowl and small game hunting.

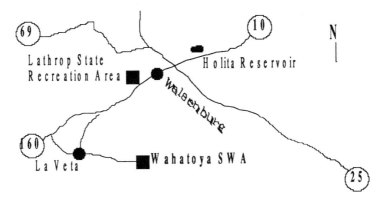

JACKSON COUNTY

Lake John covers 1,000 acres of land and 560 acres of water. It offers some excellent waterfowl and small game hunting. To get there, go west of Walden on county road 12 and follow the signs. There are camping and toilet facilities on the property.

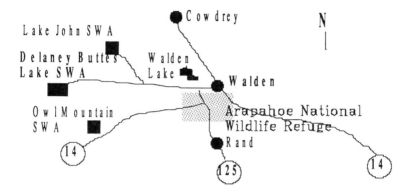

The MacNaughton Easement is 1 mile north of Walden off Highway 125. There are 2,030 acres of land in the park which features small game hunting. North Park is one of Colorado's finest high mountain parks. The area is dotted with lakes and lined with 39 miles of stream frontage. It provides excellent hunting prospects for upland birds, waterfowl, big and small game.

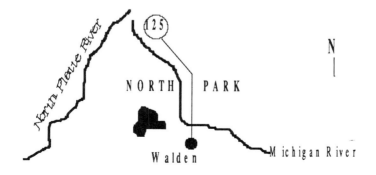

Richard SWA covers 3,820 acres of land and 6 miles of the North Platte River. It's popular with big game and waterfowl hunters. To get to the park, take county road 12 out of Walden and follow the signs.

Walden Reservoir is 1 mile west of Walden on county road 12. There are 500 acres of land and 1,000 acres of water in the park for waterfowl and small game hunting.   Owl Mountain is a SWA 15 miles southeast of Walden off Highway 14. There are 920 acres in the park. Big and small game hunting are supported.

KIOWA COUNTY

The Queens SWA covers 1,900 acres of land and over 6,000 acres of water which support waterfowl, big and small game hunting. There are boat launch, camping and toilet facilities in the park. To get there, go 5 miles west of Lamar on Highway 50 and turn north on 287 for about 15 miles.

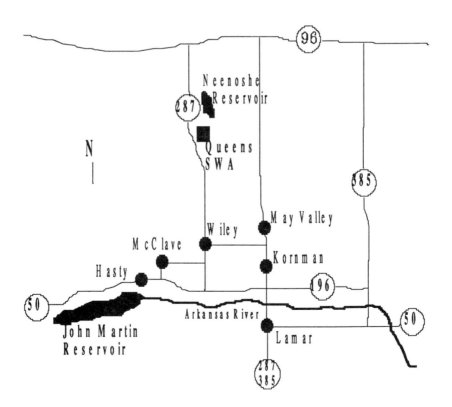

The Flagler SWA is 4 miles east of Flagler off Interstate 70. There are 570 acres of land and 160 acres of water in the park which offers waterfowl and small game hunting. Camping facilities include toilets and running water.

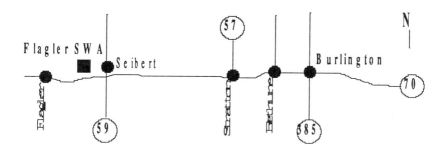

The Bodo SWA is 1 mile south of Durango Highway 550. There are over 7,500 acres in this fine park which offers both big and small game hunting.

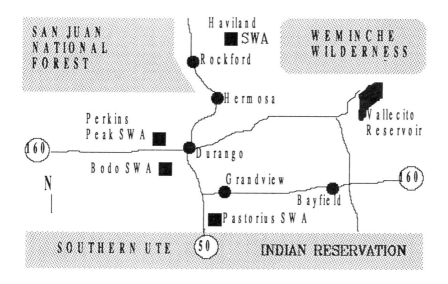

Haviland SWA is 18 miles north of Durango on Highway 50. There are 240 acres of land and 65 acres of water offering good waterfowl hunting. Camping is available in the adjacent San Juan National Forest.

The Pastorius SWA is 8 miles southeast of Durango on Highway 160. There are 90 acres of land and 50 acres of water which support waterfowl hunting.   Perins Peak is a large 5,800 acre park just 5 miles west of Durango off Highway 160. It offers excellent big and small game hunting.

LARIMER COUNTY

The Big Thompson Ponds are north of Fort Collins off Interstate 25. Exit 402 will bring you into the area which covers 51 acres of land and 15 acres of ponds for waterfowl hunting. The park has camping and toilet facilities.

Cherokee Park is one of the largest and most diverse of the State Wildlife Areas. The area includes four basic units totaling over 12,000 acres of land interspersed with about the same amount of U.S. Forest Service lands. The park is located northwest of Fort Collins and offers big and small game hunting.

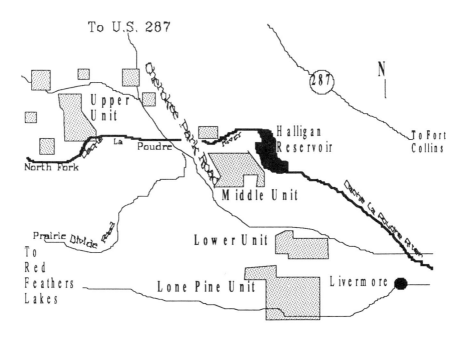

The lower and middle units range in elevation from 6,000 to 8,000 feet and provide important winter range for deer. The upper unit is above 8,000 feet and provides the rough habitat that elk prefer. The Lone Pine unit consists of terrain similar to the lower and middle units.

To reach the general area, travel 25 miles northwest of Fort Collins on U.S. 287. Exit west on Cherokee Park Road. The lower and middle units are 6 miles up the road. The upper unit is an additional 13 miles. The Lone Pine unit is 8 miles west of U.S. 287 on Red Feathers Lake Road.

The Wellington SWA is located 15 miles northeast of Fort Collins off Interstate 25. Exit at State 14 east and go north on the service road which parallels Interstate 25. The first unit is east of Cobb Lake on county road 56. The second and third units are east of county roads 60 and 64 respectively.

Each unit includes ponds and marshes which are good habitat for waterfowl, small game and pheasants. There are 2,300 acres on the property which includes camping facilities.   Hunters are required to check in and out of the park check station to assure compliance to special restrictions in the area.

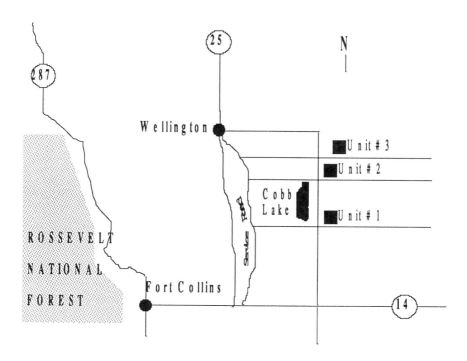

LAS ANIMAS

The Apishapa SWA features deer, antelope and small game hunting which includes quail and rabbits.   The area is located 20 miles northeast of Walsenburg off State 10.   Apishapa covers almost 8,000 acres of beautiful canyons and cedar covered plains. The Apishapa River flows through the property.

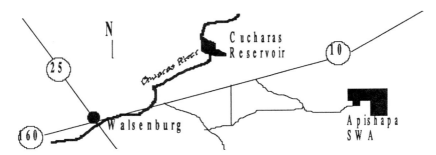

The Spanish Peaks SWA is 17 miles southwest of the town of Aguilar. The park covers over 5,000 acres of big and small game hunting habitat. Turkey hunting is a special feature of the area. There are camping and toilet facilities on the property.

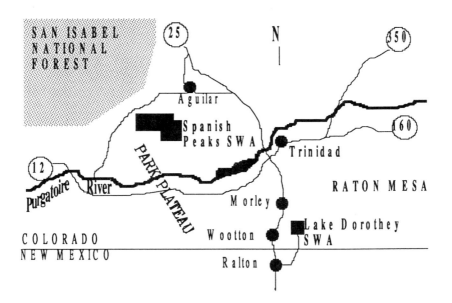

Lake Dorothey is 17 miles south of Trinidad off I-25. Take the Folsom exit at Raton, New Mexico and follow the signs back to the lake on the Colorado side of the border. There are 4,800 acres to hunt deer, small game and turkey.

LINCOLN COUNTY

The Hugo SWA is 13 miles south of the town of Hugo of I- 287. There are 3,600 acres of land and 26 acres of water in the park which features waterfowl, small and big game hunting.

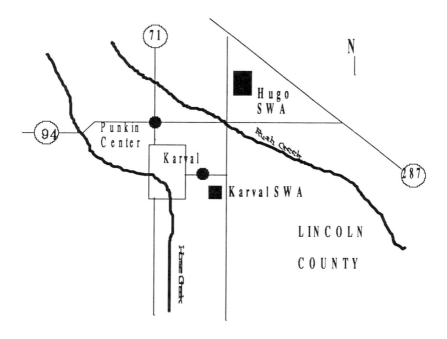

Karval Reservoir is 2 miles east of the town of Karval. The park covers 235 acres of land and 25 acres of water. Waterfowl hunting is popular on the property which includes camping and toilet facilities.

LOGAN COUNTY

There are four excellent SWAs in Logan County that are all within the same area. They are Tamarack Ranch, Duck Creek, Red Lion and the South Platte SWAs. Together, the parks cover over 16,000 acres of prime hunting habitat for waterfowl, big and small game.

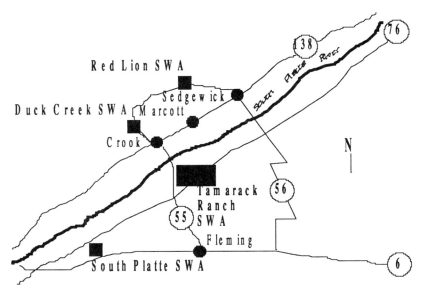

MESA COUNTY

Plateau Creek is located four miles west of Colbran off Highway 330. There are 1,350 acres of land in the park which includes camping facilities. It offers big, small and upland game hunting.

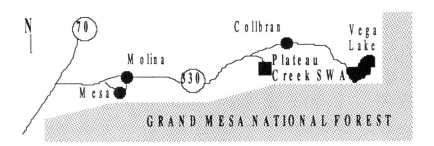

MINERAL COUNTY

Coller SWA is located 10 miles southeast of Wagon Wheel Gap. This 740 acre park straddles Highway 149 and includes camping facilities. It offers big game hunting.

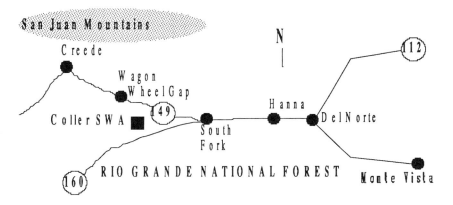

MOFFAT COUNTY

Browns Park is 50 miles northwest of Maybell off Highway 318. Exit at the Cold Spring Mountain road. There are 2,225 acres of big game land to hunt. Camping facilities are available in the park.   The Little Snake SWA is 20 miles northwest of Maybell off Highway 318. The park includes 4,680 acres, camping facilities and big game hunting.

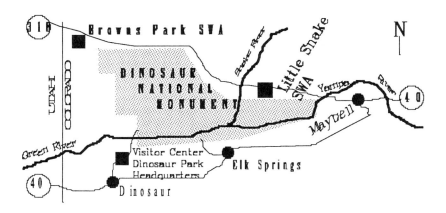

MONTEZUMA COUNTY

Narraguinnep Reservoir is a 535 acre lake that is open for waterfowl hunting. The park is located 10 miles northwest of Cortez off Highway 184. Exit at Highway 184 to the parks' entrance.

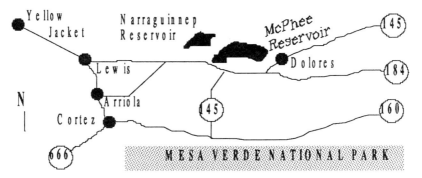

Puett and Summit Reservoirs offer waterfowl hunting 10 miles southeast of Dolores. The two lakes cover about 540 acres of water. Both are located off Highway 184. Totten Reservoir is south of Dolores off Highway 145. It covers 250 acres of water and can be used for waterfowl hunting.

MONTROSE COUNTY

Cimarron is a 6,440 acre SWA which is located about 23 miles southeast of Montrose. Exit off Highway 50 at Little Cimmaron Road to reach the park. There are some small ponds on the property which provide waterfowl hunting. Most of the hunting is for upland and big game.

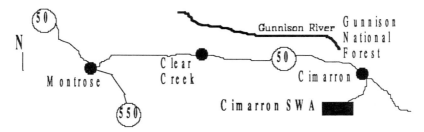

MORGAN COUNTY

The 1,450 acre Bob Elliott SWA parallels both sides of the South Platte River northeast of Brush. To reach the property, go east on U.S. 6 from Brush and turn northeast on County Road 35.5 which takes you into the main parking area.

The park is densely covered with various trees, grasses, and marshes which provide ideal habitat for many species of wildlife. The area supports small and big game hunting as well as waterfowl, pheasants and quail. Both mule and white tailed deer inhabit the park.

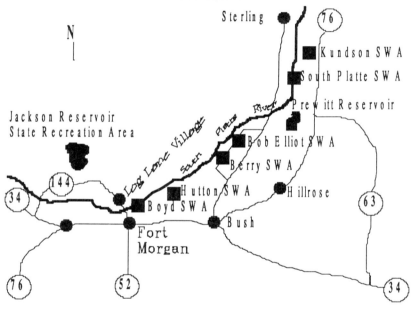

Boyd SWA is 2 miles west of Morgan. Take the county road east at Lag Lane Village into the park. If you continue up the same road, you'll reach Holton and Berry State Wildlife Areas. Each of the parks are under 200 acres and offer small game and waterfowl hunting.

Jackson Lake is surrounded by 395 acres of land that can be used for small game and waterfowl hunting. To get there, take Highway 76 northeast of Wiggins and exit north on State 39 which will take you to the south side of the lake. Follow the signs from there.

OTERO COUNTY

Rocky Ford SWA is 2 miles northwest of the town of Rocky Ford off Highway 266. There are 665 acres of land to hunt including big and small game and waterfowl. The park has camping and toilet facilities. Holly SWA is just a short distance further up the road from Rock Ford SWA. It also supports waterfowl hunting.

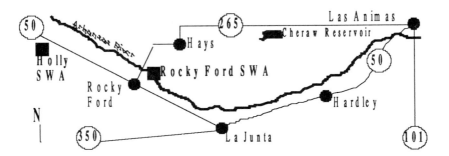

OURAY COUNTY

Billy Creek is a 5,600 acre SWA just to the east of the town of Eldredge and Highway 550. It's a popular big game hunting park and does have camping facilities.

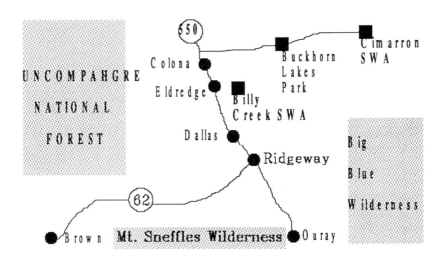

PARK COUNTY

Tarryall Reservoir is 15 miles southeast of Jefferson on the Jefferson Creek county road. The park covers 710 acres of land and 175 acres of water. It supports big game hunting and does have camping facilities.

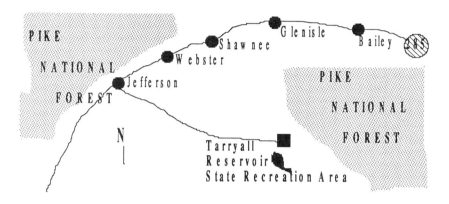

The Tomahawk SWA is located in South Park and offers 1,680 acres of big and small game hunting. The park is 7 miles north of Hartsel.

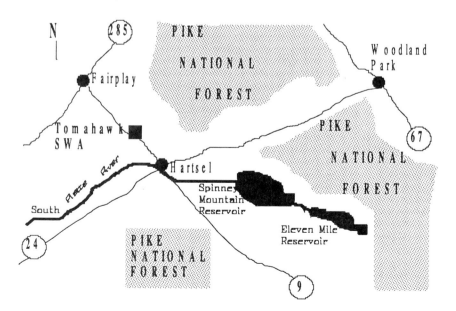

PHILLIPS COUNTY

Frenchman SWA offers 670 acres of small game and waterfowl hunting 5 miles west of Holyoke off Highway 6. Holyoke SWA is 4 miles south of Holyoke off Highway 385. Both parks are popular with upland game bird hunters.

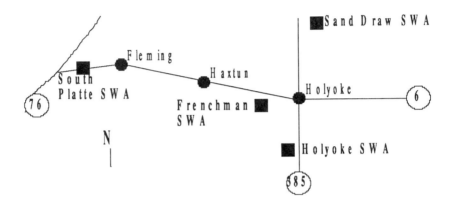

PITKIN COUNTY

The Christine and Basalt SWAs are just outside of Basalt off Highway 82. There are 1,475 acres of land to hunt in the parks. Big game hunting and, in particular, elk hunting are popular in both parks.

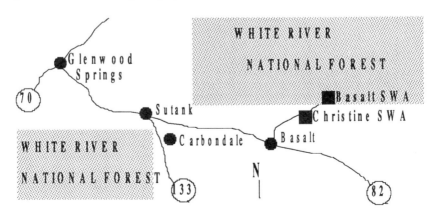

POWERS COUNTY

Clay Creek and Holly SWA cover over 1,500 acres of land and 25 acres of water. The parks are located   east of Lamar off Highway 50 and support waterfowl, big, and small game hunting. If you go 10 miles north of Lamar on Highway 149, you can hunt waterfowl on the 175 acre Thurston Reservoir.

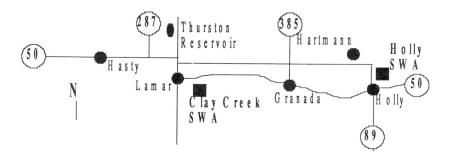

PUEBLO COUNTY

Pueblo SWA is a 8,312 acre park that includes several miles of the Arkansas River and the river inlet into the Pueblo Reservoir. The park offers duck, geese, dove, rabbit and deer hunting.

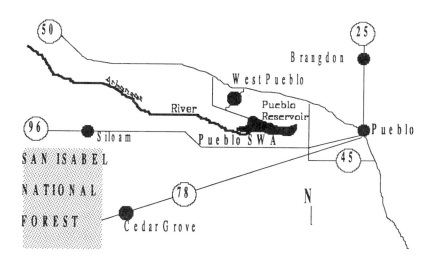

Directly to the east of the park is the 12,000 acre Pueblo State Recreation Area. It includes the 5,700 surface acre Pueblo Reservoir complete with camping, toilet and boat launch facilities.

You can access the southwest side of the park by taking Highway 96 west of the town of Pueblo. Access to the northwest side is from U.S. 50 at Swallow Run and Nichols Boulevard turnoffs.

RIO BLANCO COUNTY

Cathederal Bluffs is a 640 acre SWA located 18 miles south of Rangly off Highway 139. It offers big game hunting and camping facilities. Missouri Creek is another 10 miles south on Highway 139 with an additional 2,070 big game acres to hunt.

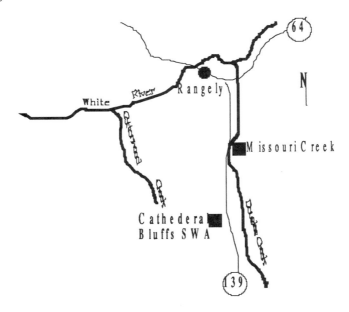

Located 13 miles southeast of Meeker on State 132 is the Oak Ridge SWA. Oak Ridge includes over 8,000 acres. There are excellent hunting opportunities for deer, elk, black bear, blue grouse, rabbits, dove and band-tailed pigeons. Camping facilities are available in the park.

Piceance SWA is 15 miles northwest of Rio Blancho. This huge 29,000 acre park supports both big and small game hunting. There are camp sites and tolet facilities on the property. Jensen SWA is 9 miles north of Meeker off highway 13. There are over 5,900 acres of land to hunt for big game.

RIO GRANDE COUNTY

The Rio Grande is just 3 miles east of Monte Vista and covers 1,450 acres of cottonwood groves and marshes. Four miles of the Rio Grande River flow through the property. The area provides ideal hunting conditions for ducks, geese, pheasants and small game animals.

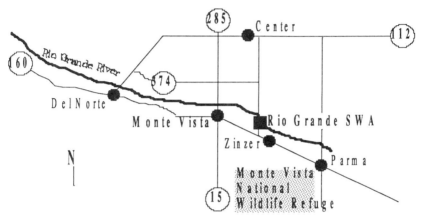

ROUTT COUNTY

Hayden Library allows big game hunting on 2,080 acres. The park is 20 miles north of Hayden on U.S. Forest Service Road 150.

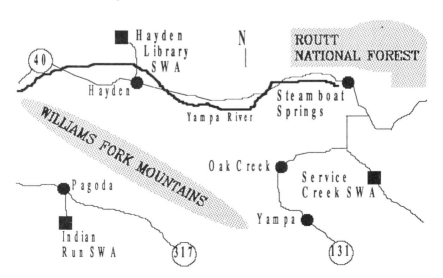

Indian Run covers 2,040 acres of land and includes camp sites with toilet facilities. The park is open to big game hunting. To get there, travel east of Hamilton on Highway 317 to Pagoda. The park entrance is 6 miles south of Pagoda.

Service Creek is a 310 acre SWA 15 miles south of Steamboat Springs. There are camp sites and toilet facilities on the property. The park supports big game hunting.

SAGUACHE COUNTY

The Cochetopa and Dome Lakes SWAs are 28 miles southeast of Gunnison. From Gunnison, travel 8 miles east on Highway 50 to Highway 114. Travel 20 miles south on 114 and exit at the SWA sign. This 2,280 acre park can be used for big and small game hunting.

Saguache Park is in the same general area as Cochetopa. The exit for the park is 20 miles south from the intersections of Highways 50 and 114. Exit on Old Highway 15 and travel south for 10 miles to Forest Service Road 787. Continue south on 787 to the park entrance. This 200 acre park offers big game hunting. Russell Lakes covers 160 acres of land and ponds and offers waterfowl hunting. The park is 10 miles south of Saguache off Highway 295.

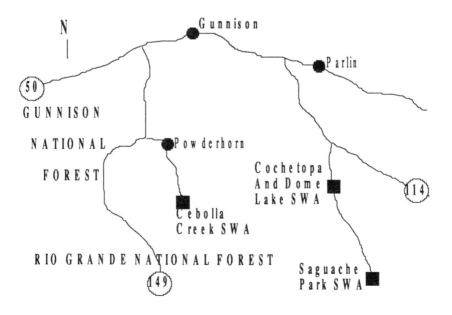

SAN MIGUEL COUNTY

Dry Creek Basin is a key winter range for deer and elk. The park contains more than 8,000 acres bordered by an additional 17,000 acres of Bureau of Land Management property adjacent to its' borders. The park offers primitive camping facilities. Drycreek is located 20 miles southeast of Naturita off Highway 141.

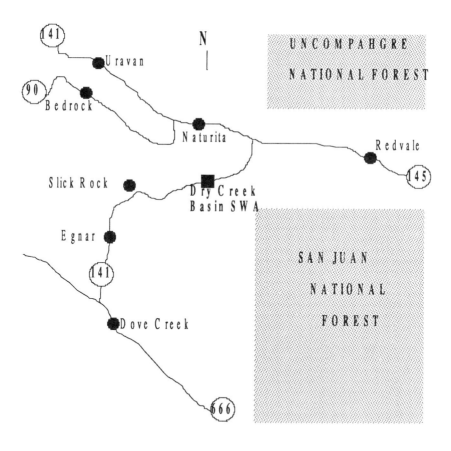

Miramonte Reservoir SWA is 17 miles south of Norwood. Travel east out of Norwood on Highway 145 and exit south on Lone Cone Road which will take you to the reservoir. The park includes a total of 510 acres of land and 810 acres of water to hunt waterfowl. There are boat launches, camp sites and toilet facilities on the property.

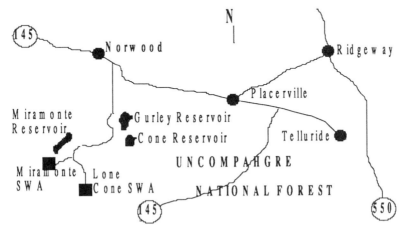

SEDGWICK COUNTY

Sand Draw is 6 miles south of Julesburg off Highway 385. There are 210 acres of land in the park which support small game hunting. Sedgewick Bars SWA is one mile east of the town of Sedgewick off Highway 138. The park offers 140 acres of small game and waterfowl hunting.

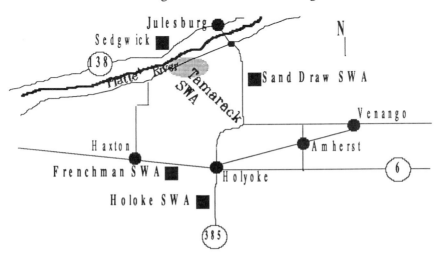

TELLER COUNTY

Sheep Rock covers 6,000 acres of land, ponds and streams to provide excellent habitat and hunting for big and small game. The park is 5 miles south of Divide off Highway 69.

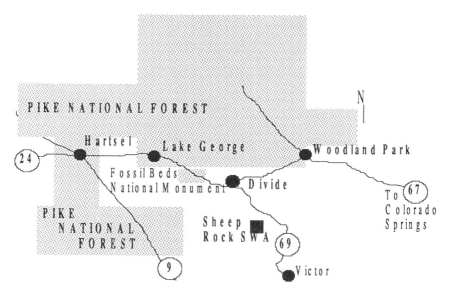

WASHINGTON COUNTY

Prewitt Reservoir is locate 9 miles northeast of Hillrose off Highway 76. There are 495 acres of land and 2,430 acres of water within the parks' boundary. Waterfowl, upland and small game hunting are allowed. There are camp sites and tolet facilities in the park.

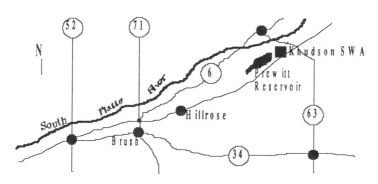

YAMPA COUNTY

The South Republic SWA includes more than 11,000 acres of land. The park is open to waterfowl, upland bird, small game and deer hunting. There are extensive camping facilities in the park which is located 20 miles north of Burlington off State 385. A variety of hunting regulations effect South Republic. Check with the Division of Wildlife before you plan your trip.

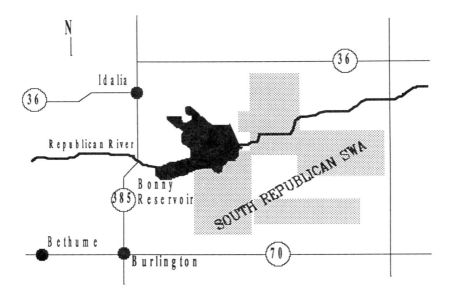

HUNTERS NOTES

p.o. box 1333, livingston, montana 59047 Ph. (406) 587-9460

GAME CARE & RECIPES

GAME CARE

Big game hunting can be a source of top quality meat. Virtually all of the so-called "wild" or "gamey" taste in game is because of poor processing by the hunter, not the intrinsic quality of the meat.

It is impossible to duplicate the exact procedures used by commercial slaughter houses when processing big game in the field. However, enough poor practices can be eliminated to make the difference negligible.

If you follow our recommended procedures, you should end up with some quality meat that you will be proud to share with your friends. The minimum equipment that you should carry is a good sharp 5 to 6 inch knife. Take along 15 feet of nylon rope for dragging and hanging your kill. Plastic bags are handy for storing the heart and liver. A supply of cheese cloth or old sheets can be used to cover the carcass to keep the flies away. A meat saw or hack saw are requisite for cutting up your animal.

YOUR BEST SHOT

The animal should be killed instantly. The best locations are the head or neck shot. If the head is to be saved for mounting or if the head-neck region are hidden, place the shot in the heart-lung area just behind the front shoulder. Be sure to stay close to the shoulder and avoid the stomach region which may allow the game to escape only to die, perhaps days later.

A third choice is a shot in the middle of the shoulder. This is just as deadly as the second choice area although more meat will be ruined by the bullet. If these areas cannot be hit, don't shoot.

Hunters should practice before the beginning of each big game season to make sure their rifles function properly. Sights and scopes can be easily jarred out of alignment and should be checked before each hunt. Avoid taking long or difficult shots. The best hunters try to stalk within easy range of the quarry and kill the animal instantly with one shot.

CLEANING BIG GAME

Cleaning should take place as soon after the kill as possible. Immediately after death, gas will begin to accumulate in the body cavity. The longer the wait, the more difficult the animal is to gut and the less desirable it is for human consumption.

If an animal has been hit in the heart or lung region, it will cause internal bleeding. Opening the carcass will rid the body of the blood. If the shot hit the head or neck, the animal's main arteries and veins at the base of the neck should be cut. It is important to remove the blood from the body as soon as possible to cool the meat.

If the head is to be mounted, bleed the animal by entering through the rib cage and severing the large veins and arteries connected to the heart.

Begin cleaning by cutting through the hide from the anus to the head. Cut down through the leg muscles to the pelvic bone. Turn the knife over and cut through the skin over the abdomen by using two fingers from the other hand to hold the intestines and stomach away from the tip of the knife. Continue cutting up through the breastbone into the neck.

The windpipe and esophagus should be severed as close to the head as possible. Tie a string tightly around the esophagus to avoid contents from contaminating the meat. Then cut around the anus and tie it with a string for the same reason.

Next, cut the thin diaphragm muscle that separates the heart-lung compartment from the main digestive tract away from the ribs. Now is a good time to remove the heart and liver. They are excellent eating and should be kept in a plastic bag for cleanliness.

Lay the animal on its side. All the contents should either fall out or can be pulled out easily. A few cuts close to the backbone may be necessary to separate organs that remain attached. The animal should then be hung by the hind legs to allow blood to drain from the body cavity and air to circulate around the body to cool it.

In the absence of a tree, fence or other object on which to hang the carcass, place logs or stones under it to keep it off the ground. This will allow the body heat to escape more easily.

In either case, prop the body cavity open with sticks and wipe the body cavity clean. If the body cavity is accidently soiled from digestive tract contents, wash it out with clean water. Water should not be used to wash the body cavity after the cavity has been dried and sealed.

The carcass should be skinned and cooled down as soon as possible. If you must drag the carcass to a base camp, leave the skin on to keep the meat clean. If the weather is warm, move the carcass to a cooler as soon after the kill as possible. If this is not possible, transport the carcass to a cool spot at camp or home.

Remove the head by cutting through the muscles at the base of the head between the skull and the first neck vertebra, then twist the head off. The meatless lower legs can be removed with a saw or by cutting through the ligaments and cartilage at joints and twisting them off.

Cover the skinned carcass with an old sheet or cheesecloth to protect it from insects and dirt. Sprinkling black pepper on exposed meat will help keep flies away.

For ease and cleanliness during the skinning process, the carcass should be hung either by the hocks or head . Cut the skin around the neck just below the head and around each leg above the hoof, then up the inside of each leg to the center cut.   Work from the top to the bottom to separate the hide from the carcass. Avoid getting hair and dirt on the carcass or cutting holes in the hide.

TRANSPORTING MEAT

Transporting a big game carcass for a few hours is seldom a problem. The carcass should be kept as clean and cool as possible. For longer trips or in warm weather, it is advisable to place bags of ice in and around the carcass to keep it cool. For trips of several hundred miles, the carcass should be butchered, frozen, packed in ice and driven or flown to its' destination.

The purpose of aging is to make the meat more tender. aging also improves upon the flavor of the meat. It is advisable not to age the carcass longer than necessary. Aging recommendations at 40 degrees are as follows:

Antelope - 3 days
Deer - 7 day
Cow Elk - 7 days
Bull Elk and Moose - l4 days

Temperatures warmer than 40 degrees will shorten the recommended aging period. If the carcass is exposed to 60 or 70 degrees weather during the day, it should be butchered and frozen in a few days. A carcass should always be aged in the shade. After aging, the carcass is ready for butchering and the freezer.

BUTCHERING BIG GAME

Deciding whether to cut up a big game animal yourself or to pay a professional butcher for the service can be a difficult decision, especially for the novice. Locker plants have the advantage of cold storage facilities for cooling and aging the carcass.

An unheated garage, porch or shed, where the carcass can hang in cool weather is required for home-aging. Aging can be omitted, but the result will be a loss of tenderness.

Butchering a big game carcass yourself will save you money. In addition, you will learn more about the anatomy and condition of the animal which will t make you a better hunter. Expect to spend one long evening completing the job of skinning, cutting and wrapping the carcass.

Required equipment for butchering meat includes a sharp knife, a sharpening stone to keep it sharp, a meat or hack saw, freezer wrapping paper, tape and a marking pen.   You will also need a large cutting board, containers for bones, meat scraps, burger or stew meat. If you don't own a meat grinder, have a butcher grind the meat scraps into hamburger for you.

Cutting up large game can be either simple or complex. Many hunters simply cut all the meat off the skeleton and have it made into hamburger, sausage, salami, jerky or stew meat.   Others prefer to cut up a big game carcass as one would cut up beef, making several kinds of steak and roasts as well as ribs and hamburger.

The decision on how to cut up a big game carcass should be based on your family's preferences for meats and to some extent, on the size of the carcass.

For example, if it's a small antelope or deer and the family uses ground meat frequently, grinding most of the meat for this use would be a good idea. On the other hand, a large elk or moose could be processed into a variety of cuts to avoid boredom on the menu.   If you choose to cut up you carcass into a variety of cuts, here is what you will need to do. Start off by hanging the carcass by the hind hocks.

Work with one part of the animal at a time. Remove one of the front legs and shoulders from the rib cage. No saw is necessary. The muscles of the shoulder can be separated and made into steaks or roasts. The shank should be ground or cut for stew meat or jerky.

Remove the other front leg and shoulder and treat it in a similar fashion. Trim as much meat as possible from the neck. It makes excellent stew or ground meat.

Remove the boneless flanks by cutting from the last rib along the loin down to the hind leg. This can be used for ground meat or jerky. On larger animals, this portion is thick enough to be used as a steak.

Next, remove each loin. Cut along the entire length of the backbone next to the dorsal spines. Then cut along the lateral backbone spines for the length of the backbone. Sever the loin where it is still attached at the small of the back.

Remove the loosely attached meat near the neck end of the loin. This meat is good for stews or ground round. The loin is most suitable for steaks. Cut crossways for thick 3/4 to 1 inch steaks.

On loins from small animals, make butterfly steaks by cutting sections about 2 inches thick. Cut the steaks in half leaving enough connective tissue to hold both halves together.

The meat on and between the ribs can be cut off with a knife and used as ground meat or jerky. To prepare ribs for barbecuing, saw the ribs into 5 - 7 inch pieces. Cut ribs into widths as desired. Ribs also can be cut into shorter pieces and used in a stew.

The tenderloin is a small muscle connected to the under side of the backbone just in front of the pelvic area. Cut it away from the backbone. It, along with the loin, is one of the most tender pieces of meat and most suitable for steaks.

Tenderloin from game can be cooked whole. Larger tenderloin may be made into butterfly steaks as previously described. Many hunters who age their carcasses remove the tenderloins early to avoid drying.

Remove the backbone just in front of the hindlegs. Separate the two hindlegs by sawing through the middle of the backbone. Remove the rump roast by cutting off the upper end of the leg. This cut should go through the ball and socket joint.

The sirloin tip is the football-shaped muscle at the front of the hind leg. Remove it next. It makes an excellent roast. Separate the large muscles of the round, upper part of the leg. These can either be cooked whole as roast or cut into steaks.

The shank of the hind leg, like that of the foreleg, contains considerable connective tissue and is best for ground or stew meat. The bones remaining also can be used. The backbone can be cut into sections and used in making soup. Bones also may be used as dog food.

GAME RECIPES

ANTELOPE FONDUE

Antelope fillets cut into 2:" cubes
salt 1 tsp
corn or peanut oil 3 cups

Marinade
vinegar 2 tbsp
brown sugar 2 tbsp
ground ginger 2 tsp
soy sauce 1/2 cup
minced garlic 1 clove

Combine ingredients for marinade. Add meat cubes, cover and marinate in refrigerator for three hours or overnight. Pour oil into fondue pot and add salt to prevent splattering. Set oven control at 425 degrees. Cover with lid and heat 10 to 15 minutes. Drain meat throroughly and cook to desired taste. Serve with a sauce. Allow 1/3 to 1/2 pounds of meat per serving.

BEAR POT RAOST

Bear meat 6 pounds
flour 1/4 cup
salt 1 tsp.
pepper 1/4 tsp.
vinegar 1 tbsp.
salt pork, diced 1/2 pound
cold water 2 cups
bay leaf 1
medium potatoes 6
carrots 6
yellow turnip 1
small onions 6

The shoulder or the lower end of the round are satisfactory cuts for pot roast. Mix together flour, salt, pepper and rub the mixture onto the surface of the meat. Put the salt port into a heavy iron or aluminum kettle or dutch oven and fry. Remove salt pork scraps and brown the bear meat in the remaining fat turning often until the entire surface is well browned. Add water, bay leaf and vinigar. Cover and let cook slowly until tender - about 3 hours. Prepare vegetables and place them around the meat after it has cooked 2 hours. When done, place roast on platter and arrange vegetables around it.

DEER HAWAIIAN STYLE

Venison steaks 2-3 pounds cut in 1" cubes
flour 1/2 cup
margarine 1/4 cup
boiling water 1 cup
salt 1 tsp.
green peppers cut in 1" squares 2 to 3
pineapple chunks 1/2 cup

Hawaiian Sauce
cornstarch 2 tsp.
pineapple juice 1/2 cup
vinegar 1/4 cup
sugar 1/4 cup
soy sauce 3 tsp.

Boil green pepper squares 10 minutes and drain. Coat meat with flour and brown in margarine. Add water and salt and simmer until meat is tender. Add pineapple and browned meat. Pour Hawaiian sauce over mixture and simmer a few minutes. Serve over Chinese noodles or rice.

DOVE HEAVEN

Whole doves 8
oranges peeled and sliced 3
bacon strips 8
port wine 1 cup
lemon juice 2 tbsp.
currant jelly 1 cup

Salt and pepper inside and outside of doves. Baste insides with lemon juice. Place orange slice into breast cavity. Cover dove breast with bacon slice and anchor with tooth picks. Close vent and place in roasting pan. In separate pan, pre-heat sauce ingredients. Roast doves in 350 degree oven for 15 to 20 minutes and baste frequently with sauce.

DUCK SUPREME

Duck, cut up 1
red wine 1 cup
chicken stock 1 can
water 1/2 cup
pickled onions 10
mushrooms 1 can
green olives 10
parsley 1 tsp.
bay leaf 1

Shake pieces of duck with flour in bag. Bring to a simmer red wine, chicken stock and water. Place duck in broth and add onions, mushrooms, olives, parsley, bay leaf, salt and pepper. Simmer 2 to 3 hours until tender.

ELK STEAK

Elk steak 2" and 2-3 pounds
butter 1/4 cup
dried garlic flakes 1/2 tsp.
thyme 1/4 tsp.
tarragon 1/4 tsp.
marjoram 1/4 tsp.
powdered mustard 5 tbsp.
port wine 3 tbsp.
black pepper 1 tsp.
currant jelly 4 tbsp.

Combine butter with garlic, thyme, tarragon, and marjoram. Melt in microwave to make simi liquid mixture. Make a paste of mustard, pepper, wine, jelly and marinate steak overnight in paste. Broil steaks, basting with herb butter mixture and remaining mustard paste until done to your taste.

GOOSE FOR CHRISTMAS

Large 5 pound goose
salt 2 tsp.

Sausage-Onion Stuffing
water 3 cups
currant jelly 1/2 cups
onion powder 1 tsp.
java black pepper 2 tbsp.
arrowroot 2 tbsp.
butter 1 tbsp.
sausage meat 3/4 pound
finely choped onions 1 cup
chopped parsley 2 tbsp.
sage 1 tsp.
milk 1/2 cup
beaten egg 1

   Wash goose well and pat dry. Sprinkle 2 teaspoons of salt inside cavity
and on the outer skin. Stuff with sausage-onion stuffing. Truss tightly and
place on rack, breast down in roasting pan.   Roast in 325 degree oven for
1 to 2 hours until light brown. Turn side up. Prick lightly with fork to allow
excess fat to un off. Continue roasting 2 hours longer or until goose is rich
golden brown and done.

GROUSE AND SAGE CHICKEN MEADOWS

Grouse or sage chicken, cut in serving pieces
white wine 2 cups
butter 1/4 cup
chopped shallots 1/4 cup
chopped parsley 1 tsp.
tarragon 1/8 tsp.
thyme 1/8 tsp.

   Marinate the grouse overnight in a mixture of 1 cup of wine, tarragon and
thyme. Place grouse, remaining wine, butter, shallots and parsley in skillet
and fry until brown (10 to 12 minutes).

GOAT AND SHEEP BOURGUIGNONNE

Mountain goat or sheep steak 2 lbs.
or tenderloin cubed
salt pork or bacon 1/4 lb.
salt 2 tsp.
freshly ground pepper 2 tsp.
dry red wine 2 cups
water 1 cup
small onions 4
fresh mushrooms

Herb Bouquet
carrot 1
chopped parsley 3 tsp.
bay leaf 1
thyme 1 tsp.
clove garlic 1

   Fry pork until crisp. Drain and save drippings. Coat meat with flour, salt
and pepper. Brown meat slowly on all sides in 2 tablespoons of drippings.
Place in heavy casserole dish with pork. Place all herb bouquet ingredients
in cheesecloth and tie with string. Boil wine, water and herb bouquet
together. Pour liquid over meat.
   Cover tightly and bake in 350 degree oven for about 2 hours or until tender.
Skim off all fat. Saute raw onions and mushrooms separately in butter. Add
onions to meat and bake and additional 30 minutes. Add mushrooms, top with
parsley and bake another 10 minutes.

PHEASANT SWEET & SOUR

Pheasant breast 2
clove garlic peeled and crunched 1
water 1 cup
soy sauce 2 tbsp.
green pepper seeded and cut in 1" squares
flour 1 cup
egg slightly beaten with 1 tbsp. water
carrot peeled

PHEASANT SWEET & SOUR (Continued)

sliced thin onion
8-oz can pineapple chunks drained (save Juice)
salt 1 tsp.
cooked rice 2 cups

Sweet & Sour Sauce
vinegar 3/4 cup
catsup 1 tbsp.
sugar 3/4 cup
soy sauce 2 tbsp.
unsweetened pineapple juice 1/2 cup
cornstarch 1 tbsp.
sherry 1/4 cup
water 1/2 cup

Place pheasant in a steamer. Steam only until meat can be removed from the bone (meat should be rare). Cool meat and cut into cubes. Roll cubes in beaten egg and then toss cubes in a paper bag with flour. Heat oil in wok or large fryingpan and cook cubes until light brown and crispy. Drain and set aside. Remove oil from pan and heat 1 tablespoon of salt and stir until brown.

Add green peppers and carrots. Stir fry about 1 minuteand then add 1 cup of water and soy sauce. Cover and steam about 3 minutes. Stir fry until liquid has evaporated. Pour in sweet and sour sauce with pineapple and meat added. Stir until meat reheated. Serves 4 over rice.

To make sweet and sour sauce, in small pan, combine vinegar, pineapple juice, water, sugar and catsup. Stir until sugar dissolves and add soy sauce. Dissolve cornstarch in sherry and stir into rest of ingredients over low heat until thickened.

RABBIT FRICASSEE

Rabbit boned and cut into small pieces
flour 1 cup
bacon strips 3
salt 1 tsp.
pepper 1/2 tsp.
chicken bouillon cube
water 1 cup
medium onions sliced into thin rings 2

In a large skillet, fry bacon until crumbly. Remove bacon from pan and place on paper towel. Save drippings in pan. In shallow bowl, mix flour, salt and pepper. Dredge rabbit in flour mixture. Fry meat over medium heat in bacon drippings turning occasionally until brown. Dissolve bouillon cubes in water and pour into skillet. Add onions, cover and simmer for 45 minutes. Serve topped with crumbled bacon.

SQUIRREL STEW

Squirrels cut up into serving pieces 3
chopped onion
water 3 qts.
tomatoes 4 cups
diced bacon 1/4 cups
diced potatoes 2 cups
cayenne 1/4 tsp.
lima beans 2 cups
salt 2 tsp.
corn 2 cups
black pepper 1/4 tsp.

Place squirrel pieces in large kettle of water. Bring slowly to a boil then reduce heat. Simmer 1 hour or until meat can be easily removed from the bones. Remove meat from bones and return meat to liquid. Add bacon, cayenne, salt, pepper and lima beans. Cook one hour. Add corn and cook 10 minutes. Serves 6 to 8.

DIRECTORY

A

B

C

ORDER FORM

You may order additional copies of *Colorado's Guide To Hunting* or *Colorado's Guide To Fishing* with a money back guarantee by sending $9.95 postage paid for each book direct to Western Publications at the following address:

Western Publications
2525 Arapahoe Avenue
Suite E4-194
Boulder, Colorado 80302